"There are certain authors worth reading simply because their words paint masterpieces that, though they are limited to black ink on a white page, simply glow with color and beauty. And, if *Your God Is Too Glorious* was merely a beautiful portrait of wordsmithing, it would be a worthwhile and deeply satisfying read. But that's not all it is. It is a portrayal of the love and humility of a God, our God, who is near to the 'least of these.' In other words, he's near to us. He's a God whom, sadly, many in the modern church have replaced with an idol of power and haughtiness. As I read it I found myself weeping for joy and repenting with gratitude. I'm sure you will too."

Elyse M. Fitzpatrick, author of *Home: How Heaven and the New Earth Satisfy Our Deepest Longings*

"If it didn't feel too obviously ironic, I would call this book glorious. This is probably not how you had the Bible stories told to you. Especially in a culture where strength is the number one qualification of its gods, this is the book I wish my Sunday school teacher had read."

Michael Horton, Westminster Seminary, California, author of *Core Christianity*

"In a landscape of a million preachers, teachers, bloggers, and podcasters all extolling the glorious plans God has for you, why would anyone read a book by a Texas truck driver telling them that their God is too glorious? Because Chad Bird has lived the dark fall from respected theological scholar to defrocked cast-out, and has found in and through his descent and redemption that the theology of the cross is not just an abstract notion but the one true gift, one that has led him from death to new life. From the ashes has emerged a prolific and original new voice, complete with battle scars and weathered humility, a voice as true and wise as any we could ever hope for, pointing us all to the Risen Lord in the least of these, where Bird is now delighted to have found a home. As we read we suspect that this is where we all belong and can only pray that God may someday lead us."

Heather Choate Davis, author, speaker, and theologian

"There are few books that combine literary genius, biblical truth, and gospel goodness. This is one of those books. With the backward message of the gospel, Chad skillfully and beautifully tells us that we are free to be ordinary, that God is hidden in the ordinary. This book will change you. This book will make you rest. Read and rejoice."

Jessica Thompson, author, speaker, and podcaster

T0023230

YOUR GOD
2ND IS TOO ED.
GLORIOUS

FINDING GOD IN THE
MOST UNEXPECTED PLACES

YOUR GOD
2ND   IS TOO   ED.
GLORIOUS

FINDING GOD IN THE
MOST UNEXPECTED PLACES

CHAD BIRD

Published by:
1517 Publishing
PO Box 54032
Irvine, CA 92619-4032

Publisher's Cataloging-In-Publication Data
(Prepared by Cassidy Cataloguing Services)

Names: Bird, Chad, author.
Title: Your God is too glorious : finding God in the most unexpected places / by Chad Bird.
Description: Second edition. | Irvine, CA : 1517 Publishing, [2022] | Previously published: Grand Rapids : Baker Books, [2018]. | Includes discussion questions. | Includes bibliographical references.
Identifiers: ISBN 9781948969796 (hardcover) | ISBN 9781948969802 (paperback) | ISBN 9781948969819 (ebook)
Subjects: LCSH: Hidden God. | Glory of God. | God (Christianity)—Omnipresence. | Faith.
Classification: LCC BT180.H54 B57 2022 (print) | LCC BT180.H54 (ebook) | DDC 231.7—dc23

Printed in the United States of America.

Cover art by Zachariah James Stuef.

To Stacy, my beloved wife

Contents

Preface

We face a major handicap in our efforts to see where God is at work. It's a congenital defect. We are accompanied by two liars everywhere we go. They are sunk, side-by-side, into our faces. Some are blue, some are hazel or brown, but they all wear the colors of the enemy. "You can't hide your lying eyes," the Eagles sang, but they weren't talking about this kind of lying. For the victims of this deceit are ourselves.

Our vision has been handicapped by the flashes of glory that have blistered our eyes. Preach, God told Isaiah; say to this people, "Keep on hearing, but do not understand; keep on seeing, but do not perceive" (Isa. 6:9). Seeing, we do not see.

For instance, in the parable Jesus told in Luke 16:19–31, we think we see the manifestation of God's good graces in the rich man. After all, this fine fellow is all decked out in purple and fine linen. His table overflows with mouthwatering cuisine. Look at his mansion, his VIP list of friends, how glamorous and carefree his life is. Our eyes tell us how obvious it is that this man is heaven's poster boy for success.

Likewise, we think we see in Lazarus the revelation of what happens to a man who lives a bad life, who is far from God. Our eyes see that impoverished street dweller, his skin crowded with oozing sores, whose mouth waters at the thought of eating even the crumbs that tumble from the rich man's table. His only friends are the flea-infested mongrels who lounge about him to lick his sores. Look at how lonely he is, how penniless, how depressing his life is. Our eyes tell us how obvious it is that this man is heaven's reject.

We see the rich man as blessed, Lazarus as cursed. The rich man as God's son, Lazarus as the devil's dog. Yet when the veil is pulled back by the hand of death, the truth is revealed: Lazarus reclines at Abraham's bosom in celestial paradise while the rich man anguishes in the flames.

Seeing we do not see, for we look through eyes that are blinded by the blazes of glory instead of opened by the Spirit's hand. We fail to see the unseen.

Together, let's learn how to see the works of God in a different way: through our ears. Our vision must be held captive by the Word of God. That Word comes through our ears; it defines divine reality, and through it we are able to see as God sees. Put your eyes into your ears and you will behold the ways and works of God. Leave your eyes in their place, assume that what you see is what really is, and no glasses, no contacts, no LASIK surgery will ever transform your eyesight into Godsight.

One

God Hiding in Plain Sight

This book is for all of us who've been fooled into believing that success is defined by accomplishments—to go big or go home, to shoot for the stars instead of binding our lives in joyful surrender to the cross of God.

It is for all the invisible saints who labor unnoticed on their little acre of the kingdom of God while the world engineers neo-towers of Babel to make names for themselves.

It is for those frightened of anonymity, who think they have to be known to matter, to be first to be of any worth, who have yet to realize that God specializes in the last, the least, the forgotten, the unfamous and infamous.

It is for refugees from religious groups that have industrialized God into a vending machine where you purchase health and wealth by emptying your silver into the God-slot, only to end up with lives vacant of glory and inundated with loss and suffering.

It is for those whose eyes are so bedazzled by beauty and power and wealth that they are blind to the treasures of heaven wrapped in the brown paper simplicities of life.

It is for rural congregations and storefront missions, hidden in the shadows of sexier megachurches, in whose humble midst lost sheep are found, broken lives are redeemed, and everlasting friendships are formed with friends in the low places of this fractured world.

This book embraces a veiled spirituality that discovers God rolling up his sleeves in the toy-strewn family rooms of stay-at-home moms, the dirty cabs of John Deere tractors, and the mop rooms of school janitors, where saints are forged in the fires of lives no one will remember except God.

This book is a call for a sweeping reorientation of our understanding of how God is at work in our lives—away from the grandiose to the simple, away from the mind-blowing to the mundane.

It is for those whose God is too glorious—too glorious to be born in a stall reeking of cattle dung, too glorious to ruin his reputation by hanging out with pariahs, too glorious to bleed out between two thugs on an executioner's stake.

The true God is glorious but in ways none of us would expect, for he hides himself beneath his opposite.

Dream Small

We were watching cartoons, or tracing the ABCs in our kindergarten class, the first time the seeds were sown in the soil of our minds. Maybe while our moms and dads were bouncing us on their knees, they told us that we would do great things. And all the while we were growing up, this mindset grew up with us. It molded our perception of what matters, formed our understanding of what would put a smile on our faces and an exclamation point at the end of our lives.

I was eighteen years old when it fully blossomed within me. I began to draw up the blueprint of my future. What I didn't realize was this: I was planning how to go astray for the next twenty years of my life.

I began to dream big, to go full steam ahead, fueled by ambition. That's what my culture had taught me, after all, what I had come to believe so firmly that I never for a moment questioned its validity. We're told, whatever path we follow, to be all that we can be, to earn trophies that serve as icons of what's made our lives worth living. Each chapter in our biography should be something to boast about: "The Year My Football Team Won State," "When I Graduated with Honors," "How I Landed a Job with a Fortune 500 Company," "My Promotion to Management."

Sometimes, for some people, these big dreams do come true. Most of the time, for most people, they don't. We, along with our dreams, careen off the highway and end up stuck in a ditch along the road to glory. I went astray for two decades in the pursuit of my ambitions. I drove myself to be an accomplished person. My life had to be awesome. I chased down the career I wanted and clawed my way up to the position I coveted. I pursued a degree, then another degree, then still yet another, until I knew more about my PhD studies than the details of my children's everyday lives. I could tell you Rabbi Oshaya's exegesis of the Hebrew in Genesis 1:1 in *Bereshit Rabbah*, but I had no clue what my daughter's favorite stuffed animal was.

When my big dreams came true, when I reached the fabled end of the rainbow, I found a pot of gold—fool's gold.

If I could rewind my life and go back twenty years, I would dream small and relish the joys of an unaccomplished life. "Make it your ambition to lead a quiet life," Paul urges (1 Thess. 4:11 NIV). This is arguably one of the most un-American verses in the Bible. Those words have become almost a mantra for me. I must say them over and over to silence the lifelong indoctrination I have received from a culture that idolizes those who do big things and urges us all to do likewise. "Make it your ambition to lead a quiet life." In other words, make it your ambition not to let "awesome" define your life, dictate your relationships, weigh the importance of who you are, or guide you in discerning how and where God is found.[1]

To lead a quiet life doesn't mean that you lower your expectations as much as you lower your gaze. Instead of looking up to the next accomplishment, the next rung on the ladder, you look down at the daily life you live, the children God has given you, the spouse by your side, your aging parents, your dear friends, the poor and needy—all those "little things" you miss when you're always looking up to the "next big thing" in your life.

Likewise, instead of looking up for God in emotionally electrifying mountaintop experiences, you'll discover he is the Lord of the lowlands, transfigured by simplicity and suffering. He prefers to sit with the lonely, weep with the mourner, and wander the halls of the ICU. Instead of looking for God in the high and mighty things of this world, you'll find him tucked into the smallest crevices of life: swimming in the tears of the widow, enthroned upon a quarter-sized piece of bread from the altar, laughing in the toddler's voice as he plays in the sandbox. Instead of waiting to be wowed by God in mighty displays of his omnipotence, you'll find that power compressed into weak, unimpressive vessels like a graying preacher who shepherds a flock of Iowa farmers on the outskirts of a town no one's ever heard of.

Midnight Vision in a Hospital Bed

Our eyes are so accustomed to looking up that we don't readily see the work of God in these lowlands and shadowlands. So sometimes the Lord takes away our eyesight altogether. When we can't see, we see most clearly. The darkness illumines our minds. This happened to me one night in a hospital bed.

It's the Fourth of July. I'm fourteen years old. Adjacent to my childhood country home is a field littered with clods of dirt and wheat stubble. While the grownups lean against the wire fence, sip iced tea, and swap stories and laughs, another boy and I are all business. We have matches and explosives—two gifts from the great god Testosterone. Before long, booms and fiery shrills sing their song into the warm summer night. Two young boys, down in the dirt, playing with fire, celebrating their independence.

But one firework is stubborn. A single fuse runs from one tiny pillar to the next, designed to set off a series of blazing, colorful shots. But the fuse keeps burning out. So I get down on one knee to relight it. But still it won't cooperate. Frustrated, I decide to move to the other side and work it from that angle. As I do, for a split second, my face passes over it. And the powder ignites.

The ball of fire slams into my face directly between my eyes. I'm rolling in the dirt, screaming. My eyebrows and lashes are incinerated, my hair smoking. My face is a constellation of dark stars branded into the skin. Both my eyes are painted black with it. And there is the searing pain, which is worse than anything I've experienced in my young life.

But if I'm scared, it's nothing compared to the terror my mom and dad feel as they drive me from one hospital to another that night, wondering if their son will ever see again.

Surgery to scrape away the powder from my eyes is scheduled for the morning. All night long, my mom sits on the chair a few feet from my bed. And she transforms that simple room into a temple of prayer. She begs aloud, nonstop, through the small hours of the night, for God to have mercy upon her boy. Jesus gets no rest. She shakes God awake and challenges him, Jacob-like, to a wrestling match. And he delights to let her win.

On July 5, as the sun rises, one of the many undeserved miracles in my life rises as well. The powder covering my eyes began to dissolve through the night. The doctors examine me and leave my room scratching their heads. The surgery is canceled. And a few hours later I am released to recover at home.

That was three decades ago. Today, if you look closely at my left eye, you'll see one tiny speck of black lodged within the whiteness. It's the gunpowder of my reckless youth, a relic of the night when I first caught a glimpse of how we see, through our ears, the Father's counterintuitive means of infiltrating our lives.

It is not the unexpected healing I'm talking about. I mean that God chose to reveal himself in the midnight of a hospital room, to a blinded country boy, by means of his mother's prayers, in the thick of fear and pain and a gut-wrenching feeling that life as I knew it would never be the same. No one was happy. There was nothing good about this night. It was darkness not light, grief not joy. It was one of the longest, worst, most painful nights of my life. Yet, looking back over the years, it was precisely then that I saw, through my ears, for the first time, God at work. He chose to let me see while my eyes were burned shut. He let me see him veiled in my mother's prayers, swaddled in my fears, holding me in the horrible mess of my accident as only a Father can.

May All Your Expectations Be Frustrated

> May all your expectations be frustrated, may all your plans be thwarted, may all your desires be withered into nothingness, that you may experience the powerlessness and poverty of a child and sing and dance in the love of God who is Father, Son, and Spirit.[2]

This benediction, written by Larry Hein, the spiritual director of Brennan Manning, is beautifully absurd. It does come partially true in our lives, but not in a way that has us belting out hallelujahs. Spitting profanities, perhaps, but not shouting praises.

Our expectations are frustrated by everything from sinking marriages to rising flood waters. Our plans are thwarted by job offers that don't materialize and children who always seem too busy to call home. Our desires wither into nothingness because we suffer through bouts of depression, our health fails, or the economy atrophies. We experience the "powerlessness and poverty of a child," but you won't spy most of us singing and dancing in the love of God; rather we wring our hands as we stare at the heap of unpaid bills littering our kitchen table.

Thomas Hobbes famously said that the life of man is "solitary, poor, nasty, brutish, and short."[3] Perhaps Hobbes is too much of a downer for us, but on the flip side, we're also not naive enough to imagine that "happily ever after" is true outside of fairy tales. That's not the way things go down in the real world. None of our day-to-day homes glow with the surreal light of a Thomas Kinkade painting.

Things don't turn out the way we imagined they would. Dream jobs can be a nightmare at times. Even Love Boat marriages can go the way of the Titanic. No one in Hollywood or Nashville knows our name. We never bask in our fifteen minutes of fame. Instead, we settle into a decidedly predictable life that is sometimes happy, often hard, and occasionally quite brutal. Hein's benediction rings true: our expectations are frustrated, our plans are thwarted, our desires wither into nothingness.

In other words, our lives are exactly the kind of lives that God gets excited about.

The more unimpressive our jobs are, the more lackluster our bio, the more we feel like we're just a name on a list or a face in the crowd, the more we are the perfect venues for God's ongoing work in this world. If God is anything, he is a God who has a thing for the normal. He'll stroll right past bikinied Miss Universe to crown the homely girl with acne and braces. He is a God who turns our every expectation inside out.

The Scriptures are packed with illustrations of this tendency. To begin with, God goes out of his way to handpick the wrong people for his most important missions. The Bible is like the HR Handbook from Hell. Here's everything you should *not* do when looking for the perfect candidate for a position. Need a woman to become the mother of a promised son? Instead of choosing a robust twenty-five-year-old, the Lord taps a post-menopausal, wrinkled, ninety-year-old named Sarah for the job. She doubles over laughing when God brings it up. A few months later, she's shuffling about with her walker while shopping for maternity dresses. Need someone to lead the emancipation of slaves from the most powerful nation on earth, as well as to serve as the spokesperson for these oppressed people? Rather than choosing the ancient equivalent of a Navy SEAL or a quick-tongued Secretary of State, God handpicks a stuttering eighty-year-old shepherd named Moses who's been on the lam for forty years after beating a man to death.

Book after book, from Genesis to Revelation, the Lord demonstrates that he shuns the tried-and-true methods of an orthodox headhunter. He sends men and women on errands they are ill-qualified to fulfill. And nothing has changed in today's world. He continues to buck our manmade religious systems by inserting men and women into them who don't meet our qualifications. But they meet God's. He's delighted to use them in his kingdom to show all of us that it's not by brainpower or brawn but by the Spirit of love that the Father gets things done.

But this only scratches the surface of God's revolt against all the rules we concoct to govern divine behavior in our world. He strolls defiantly past the "No Trespassing" signs we nail up to control where he goes and what he does. Not only does he select the wrong people for his big missions but he gives huge roles in the biblical story to men and women who have fallen through the cracks in the world. These are Saints John and Jane Doe. They're nobodies who don't even merit a footnote in the history books. Like a young, kidnapped slave girl in ancient Syria. She was nothing. Just one more foreign servant. Unnamed, disposable, forgettable. Yet by her bold confession of God's healing work back home in the land of Israel, her famous master, General Naaman, embarked on a journey that involved international politics, miraculous healing, and an everlasting display of the power of Yahweh over the ravaging effects of leprosy. And it all was possible because of a Jane Doe, because of a girl whose only fame was anonymity.

This Jane is no different from the mother trying to corral her three children while pushing a cart through Wal-Mart, the high school teacher who's devoted her whole life to teaching algebra and geometry to yawning teens, or the undocumented worker we pay under the table. Though these people may see themselves as insignificant, they loom large in the eyes of our Father. Like the Israelite servant girl, they are the masks of our Lord by which he is active in our world to accomplish his good and gracious will.

God hides in plain sight. In our world, on our streets, in the back alleys and warehouses and boardrooms that look nothing like God's hangouts. He's dressed up as the misfits who embarrass us and the tollbooth workers we pass by unnoticed. And he's beneath our skin too. He has sunk himself into our unglamorous lives that there he might do what he does best: give, love, serve, help, and pray. The little things we do—like pouring cereal for our sleepy children before school, driving a delivery truck to keep businesses rolling, visiting a friend who's laid up in the hospital—these seemingly little things are divine deeds over which angels rejoice. The evening news will never report on them. The church newsletter won't mention them. No one will upload a YouTube video about them that goes viral. Yet that's their hidden beauty: unnoticed by earth, applauded by heaven. To us they seem as natural and boring as watching the grass grow. But to God, they are his humble, holy niche in a world blinded by bigger, better, bolder.

The Lord's incognito way of infiltrating the commonalities of life and infusing them with a divine purpose is not limited to our humanity. He's active not only in lackluster people but also in lackluster things and places. Sometimes, in fact, these things and places are not only lacking in glory but are positively bizarre. They're the last place one would suppose the Lord of heaven would be found on earth.

The Scriptures, especially the Old Testament, parade before us example after example of this. For instance, God hangs out in inhospitable spots. He chooses godforsaken places as the venues in which to teach his people that he won't forsake them. For instance, in the desert wilderness of the Sinai peninsula, for four long decades, Yahweh taught his people how to live by faith in his Word of promise. The five foundational books of the Bible—Genesis, Exodus, Leviticus, Numbers, and Deuteronomy—were all written by Moses here. The covenant of the law was enacted here. The priesthood, the tabernacle, and many promises of the Messiah all originated in this place where death was everywhere. Later, God would compel David, Elijah, and even Jesus into the wilderness in order that there they might live by faith in the Word of their Father. In the desert, not in a garden, God did his best work among his people. It is no different today. When it feels like we're in a place forsaken by God, when it seems our lives are a barren wilderness full of nothing but disappointments, as we drag ourselves from one oasis to the next—precisely in that wilderness of suffering, when it feels like God is most absent, he is most present in our lives.

The Old Testament stories also focus on how the Lord chooses to heal us through remedies that are far from wonder drugs. Yahweh writes prescriptions that are unorthodox. When his people suffer snakebite, he doesn't administer an antivenom. He bids his people stare at a bronze replica of a snake attached to a pole. Those suffering from leprosy are cleansed by blood and water applied to their skin. Even a dead man is raised to life when he's dropped into a grave full of a prophet's bones.

But above all else, God heals, cleanses, forgives, and makes alive through blood. No pharmaceutical company would ever market God's remedies. They aren't supposed to work. But they do. They work not because they are imbued with magical properties but because the restorative Word of the Lord is in them. The bronze snake, the water, the blood, the bones—all of this stuff, this earthly matter—are infused with grace and power by the same God who spoke creation into being from nothing.

The healing agents that God uses today for society's most sinister ailments work the same way. I'm not talking about cancer or AIDS but deeper spiritual maladies such as loss of identity, addiction to violence, widespread fear, and despair. These evils are tearing our society apart, as well as individuals and families. The Lord's medicine for these is not outwardly spectacular or even psychologically thrilling. It's still plain stuff: water and blood, a body on a tree, a piece of bread in the mouth. Yet these ordinary-looking receptacles are pregnant with God. Spilling over with the Creator's life-bestowing love. As in the Old Testament, so in the New; divine healing always comes veiled in the most generic packaging.

These are the things that God gets excited about—the nonexciting, inglorious things. This is how God works. It'll feel like an ambush at times. But that's only because we're too busy looking up for God instead of down. He's right there. Down in the dirt. Down in the ungodlike. Down in the lowliness, the simplicity, the plain elements of the world that are easily despised and forgotten.

These Old Testament stories that illustrate God's backward ways of engaging us in the world—then and now—are all preambles to the Lord's ultimate revelation. Genesis to Malachi is one long drumroll that summons the cosmos to stand at attention before the climactic unveiling of the glory of God.

And there it is, in a dying man. Soldiers gamble for his clothing. His closest friends have skulked away. His fiercest enemies spit insults in his face. Even a fellow condemned man mocks him. There is nothing, not one iota, of obvious God stuff going on here. It looks like hell. No one would walk outside Jerusalem to this spot of public execution, stand at the foot of this man's cross, look up, and say, "There is the glory of the Almighty. There is the unveiling of who God is, how God works, how he comes to us." The opposite would be said. "Looks like the devil's work. There is the shame of failure."

Seeing God on the cross, we do not see. That is, unless our spiritual eyes have been transferred to our ears. Unless we see him through the prophecies of Isaiah about the Servant who would be "despised and rejected by men; a man of sorrows and acquainted with grief; and as one from whom men hide their faces" (Isa. 53:3). The Servant who would be "pierced for our transgressions; he was crushed for our iniquities; upon him was the chastisement that brought us peace, and with his wounds we are healed" (v. 5). If the Word of God, not the vision of our eyes, defines what is real, then we shall really see God on the cross. We shall bask in glory where no glory is to be seen. On the cross, and only on the cross, the scales shall fall from our eyes so that we finally get it:

> God chose what is foolish in the world to shame the wise; God chose what is weak in the world to shame the strong; God chose what is low and despised in the world, even things that are not, to bring to nothing things that are, so that no human being might boast in the presence of God. (1 Cor. 1:27–29)

The cross is God's veiled unveiling. It is his absent presence. It is heaven dressed up as hell. The cross defines how God has always worked and always will. This is a radical, life-changing realization.

Beginning in Genesis, and continuing even now in our own lives, is the God of the cross. The Lord who chooses losers to win, the last to be first, the ugly to be gorgeous, the simple to contain the profound. He slipped into our world in a Bethlehem feed trough. He conquered the cosmos by suffering defeat in death. He made his life our own by letting humanity murder him.

He will not work the way we expect him to. Whatever seems to us as the right and proper way for God to engage our world—he will do the opposite. He's the kind of God who embarrasses us in all the right ways.

We need a complete reorientation of how we see God at work. That's what the Old Testament gives us. It's a carbon copy of our world, where run-of-the-mill people get hijacked by God to do things way outside their comfort zone. It's full of stories like ours: where the streets are full of violence, husbands and wives drive each other crazy, kids don't keep their noses clean, and people labor in thankless jobs. And precisely there God hides his kingdom. The mystery of where God is found in our world is that he's not where he's supposed to be.

But where he is—in the underwhelming simplicities of this world—he is present to give our lives meaning and purpose. When God strips away all our adult notions of how he is active among us, we can finally "experience the powerlessness and poverty of a child and sing and dance in the love of God who is Father, Son, and Holy Spirit."[4]

Discussion Questions

1. What are some ways, both subtle and obvious, that our culture programs us to think that life is all about accomplishing big, impressive things? How does this attitude influence our decisions about school, careers, relationships, money, and other aspects of life?

   _____

   _____

   _____

2. Read 1 Thessalonians 4:9-12. Paul urges Christians "to aspire to live quietly" (ESV) or "to make it your ambition to lead a quiet life" (NIV). What would such an "ambition" (really an anti-ambition) look like in a Christian's life? What does it mean to "lower your gaze" instead of "lower your expectations"?

   _____

   _____

   _____

3. The benediction by Larry Hein speaks of "your expectations…your plans…your desires." Read Psalm 37:4, Proverbs 14:12, and Romans 7:14-20. How do these passages help us to understand this part of the benediction? Read Matthew 5:3 and 2 Corinthians 12:7-10. How do these passages relate to the experience of "the powerlessness and poverty of a child"?

   _____

   _____

   _____

4.   Reflect on these words: "If God is anything, he is a God who has a thing for the normal." For instance, what normal objects did the Lord use to create Adam and Eve (Genesis 2:7, 22)? What common object did God use to part the Red Sea (Exodus 14:16)? What everyday job did both Moses and David have before the Lord called them to lead his people (Exodus 3:1; 1 Samuel 16:11)? What are some other examples of normal ways or common people that the Lord used in the past and still does today?

_____

_____

_____

5.   What does it take for a person to be considered important, to be noticed by the world? How is the Lord different? To whom does he look? Read Isaiah 57:15; 66:2; 1 Samuel 2:7-8; Psalm 34:15-18. According to Colossians 3:3, who or what does God see when he looks at us?

_____

_____

_____

6.   The Sinai desert and Judean wilderness were godforsaken places, yet God used these inglorious locations to form and shape his people. Read Psalm 42. How does this prayer give expression to the longing and hope of believers in the wilderness? According to Deuteronomy 8:1-5, how did God use Israel's time in the wilderness to shape them?

_____

_____

_____

7. What does the Lord use to heal the Israelites bitten by serpents (Numbers 21:4-9)? To purify a person made unclean by contact with a corpse (Numbers 19)? To remove the skin disease of Naaman (2 Kings 5:1-14)? In each of these, God doesn't just speak joins his word to an element of creation. How does he still work the same today?

    _____

    _____

    _____

8. Read 1 Corinthians 1:18-31, especially verses 27-29. How does this interpret the cross of Jesus? Talk about how the cross defines how God has always worked in a seemingly backward manner when dealing with humanity.

    _____

    _____

    _____

Two

Friends in Low Places

Take I-76 west out of Philadelphia about half an hour, then meander down a couple of highways heading north, and you will arrive at a national historic site named Hopewell Village. This 884-acre iron plantation, founded in 1771, was once a booming industry. A variety of products were manufactured there, including cannons and mortar shells for the Continental Army. Its original owner was not only the ironmaster and a member of the Pennsylvania Assembly but a militia colonel and deputy quartermaster general in the Revolutionary War. When George Washington's troops were stationed at Valley Forge in the winter of 1777–78, he provided a thousand barrels of flour to feed the starving men. He was related by marriage to Betsy Ross, who stitched the first American flag, as well as to three of the signers of the Declaration of Independence. In his heyday, this man was wealthy and successful, standing shoulder-to-shoulder with the first leaders of the United States.

His name was Mark Bird. He was the great-grandfather of my own great-grandfather. And he was the closest my family has ever gotten to achieving anything close to fame.

The generations of my family after Mark Bird passed from history unnoticed by the world. They migrated from the woodlands of Pennsylvania to the open country of central Texas, where they labored in cotton fields, on construction sites, in oil field supply warehouses. They were ordinary citizens, scraping together a modest living with callused hands. They raised families and sunk deep roots into the Texas soil.

My great-grandfather, grandfather, father, and I share a common personality trait: we think change is a dirty word. We love stability. None of us are gamblers or risk-takers. We are men steeped in our own traditions. We have our churches, our circle of friends, our very regimented daily schedules that give our lives a predictability that others may find boring but we find reassuring.

If God wants us in situations and circles of people outside our comfort zones, then he's going to have to drag us there kicking and screaming.

Over the last ten years, that's exactly what he's been doing with me. A little over a decade ago, I was living the life I had plotted out for myself. I was a professor of the Old Testament, living in campus housing at a conservative seminary in the Midwest, surrounded at work and home by likeminded Christians, the vast majority of whom were involved in church-related vocations. It was a safe, insular, black-and-white kind of life.

Today, I drive an eighteen-wheeler up and down the streets of an industrial section of San Antonio, Texas, surrounded by impoverished neighborhoods plagued by drugs and violence. I deliver freight to customers whose lives are the stuff of country music songs. They include ex-cons and recovering addicts, rednecks, bikers, even a former professional wrestler. As I've gotten to know them over the years, they've divulged personal stories of everything from their stint in prison, to the summer they blew vast amounts of money on strippers, to their struggles to reconnect with estranged children. They're people I never would have bumped into on a seminary campus. They are religious outsiders.

And yet God has used these men and women to teach me more about himself than I ever learned in an academic setting.

The teachers who have the greatest impact on our lives are not always standing in pulpits or guiding us through Romans during a Sunday morning Bible study. They've written no books, earned no degrees, wouldn't be invited to lecture at a Christian university. They are strangers to the religious system. They lack the credentials to garner interest among churchgoing people. They don't speak Christianese.

In fact, if we're honest with ourselves, when we look at these folks, they just don't seem to be the right kind of people to believe, much less have anything of importance to teach us about the Lord. If the Lord has friends, it wouldn't be these people.

And yet they are. God has friends in low places. He gives wisdom to those the world deems fools. He grants simple faith to people wrestling with twisted lives and scarred pasts. He puts prophets under interstate bridges and preachers on forklifts. The more the Lord has strong-armed me outside my Christian comfort zone, the more I have learned of Christianity from these outsiders. And the more I learn from them, the more I realize that this is part of God's way of hiding in our world. He cloaks himself in the garb of people who don't have "church clothes."

It's taken me years—and concrete experiences—to see this. To break down my prejudices. But that's part of the work of the Spirit in our lives. He is reconfiguring our vision to see that to which we are usually blind. He's teaching us to reevaluate our perception of what kind of people God might use to speak his Word to us. The Spirit opens our eyes to the fact that every day, in every encounter, the person in front of us may be the Lord's mouthpiece. In this unexpected place, in this humble person, in this seemingly unspiritual setting, the Lord may be hiding to reveal a profound truth to us.

He not only does this now. It's been our Lord's mode of operation from the beginning. Just ask the two Israelite spies who were taught the fear of the Lord by a Gentile woman in a Jericho whorehouse.

Theologian in the Jericho Brothel

The two young men who strolled into the high-walled city of Jericho must have looked like a couple of wide-eyed country boys walking down the Vegas strip. Their entire life had been spent in the boondocks of the Sinai peninsula. Sand and rocks. Tents and sheep. The same weary faces day in and day out. Now here they were, mesmerized by sights and smells and sensations that were as novel to them as snow in the Sahara. They were on a mission of espionage. They were secret agents of the Israelite army, sent by Joshua to spy out any weaknesses in this ancient fortress.

But as it turns out, they harbored some weaknesses of their own. "They went and came into the house of a prostitute" (Josh. 2:1). And I doubt they were there to pass out religious tracts.

When the city authorities caught wind of the real reason these two strangers were in town, they came pounding on Rahab's door, demanding she hand over the men. What they hadn't counted on was being outsmarted and outmaneuvered by this wise woman. She concealed the spies beneath stalks of flax on her roof, then informed the authorities that the men had snuck out the gate right before sunset. If they chased them now, she urged, they'd surely catch up with them. So off they went in hot pursuit.

Why did Rahab mislead the authorities? Reports of what the Lord had done for his people had been the talk of the town. How he had dried up the waters of the Red Sea, given them victory over foreign armies, and was soon to give them the very land upon which they were now standing. "The fear of you has fallen upon us," she told the spies, "[and] all the inhabitants of the land melt away before you" (v. 9). Then she confessed, "The LORD your God, he is God in the heavens above and on the earth beneath" (v. 11).

Rahab may have been a prostitute in Jericho, but she was secretly a daughter of Yahweh.

The biblical story has a dry sense of humor. The punchlines are delivered with such a straight face that the joke often goes over the heads of the über-pious. Or maybe they're just afraid to laugh. Every time I read this tale of two spies, a brothel, and a hooker named Rahab, I can't help but chuckle at the backward ways in which God gets his children out of jams. And the unlikely people he uses to do so.

These two Israelite men were religious insiders—what we'd call churchgoers. Deacons in the Israelite congregation. Bible-toting believers. They attended Sabbath services at the tabernacle. They chanted the sacred psalms. Moses himself had been their preacher. Yet here they were, being instructed in the wonder-working ways of Yahweh by a woman in the sex industry. In a city in which they expected to find nothing but pagan enemies destined for the sword, they discovered a friend of God who saved their necks and taught them some theology to boot.

When the Israelite army eventually rushed over the rubble of the collapsed walls of Jericho, Joshua commanded the two soldiers to go and rescue the woman who had earlier rescued them. They "brought out Rahab and her father and mother and brothers and all who belonged to her" (6:23). As Hebrews says, "By faith Rahab the prostitute did not perish with those who were disobedient" (Heb. 11:31). Her faith had also been active in love. She not only spared the two spies but arranged to have her whole family kept safe during the ensuing demolition of her hometown.

What later happened to Rahab is the stuff of biblical irony. Jericho's prostitute was not only Israel's rescuer but became an adopted member of the people of God. "She has lived in Israel to this day," the Bible says (Josh. 6:25). But that's not all. A man named Salmon from the tribe of Judah made Rahab his wife. Together they had a son named Boaz, who himself wed a Gentile woman named Ruth (Ruth 4:13). And Ruth became the great-grandmother of King David (vv. 21–22), from whose family tree Jesus would be born.

In a turn of events no one could have forecast, a Gentile woman who made her living having sex with strangers, who believed in the one true God, became a teacher in Israel and one of the mothers of the Messiah. The blood of a religious outsider pulsed through the veins of the virgin's Son.

Membership in the Religious Club

As we work our way through the biblical story, we find time and again that card-carrying members of the religious community are not necessarily Exhibit A of fidelity and piety. Often it's the exact opposite. Israel is the "treasured possession" of Yahweh (Exod. 19:5), but what do they themselves treasure? Military muscle, fat bank accounts, and a whole pantheon of puny gods empty of deity. There is hardly a page in the Old Testament that doesn't have a clothesline stringing up the dirty laundry of God's elect.

But the single deeper problem is not identical to the multitude of surface problems. We tend to fixate on the scandals of skirt-chasing Samson, coup-launching Absalom, and idol-building Jeroboam, but they are outward symptoms of a foundational illness. The problem was not simply a loose sexual ethic or an ongoing flirtation with false deities.

The deeper problem, which manifested itself in these outward evils, was this: a stubborn refusal to listen to and believe in the Word of God. All of Israel's sins began in their ears.

Like a broken record, the prophets preached, "Hear the Word of Yahweh." Believe in him. Follow him. Give heed to his Word. Jeremiah says, "From the day that your fathers came out of the land of Egypt to this day, I have persistently sent all my servants the prophets to them, day after day. Yet they did not listen to me or incline their ear, but stiffened their neck" (Jer. 7:25–26). The original Hebrew says that God was "daily rising early and sending [the prophets]." God is saying, as it were, "Look, Israel, I roll out of bed every morning at the crack of dawn and the first thing I do is throw another prophet your way." And the first thing Israel does is stick headphones in its ears to blare the music of disobedience.

This means that the chief problem for Israel is the same one we face in the church today. It's not scandals among the leadership, apathy in the pews, or irrelevance to a secular culture. Our chief problem is and will always be unbelief. An unbelief made possible by deafness to the Word of Yahweh. A deafness made possible by pride. And a pride made possible, all too often, by the assumption that we're good with God because our names are on a church's membership roster. Outward attachment to a religious institution is no guarantee of an inward attachment to the God of the cross. Indeed, as the Jews in Jesus's day claimed to be God's favorites because Abraham was their father, today the temptation is to claim that we are God's favorites because we're in the club called Christianity.

To counter this club mentality, to remind us that external affiliation with the church is not the same as inward belief in his saving Word, God has a habit of introducing us to women like Rahab. And men like Willy.

King of the Double-Wide Trailer

I met Willy when I began my truck driving career in the oil and gas fields of the Texas panhandle. We worked the night shift together, pulling tankers up and down the serpentine dirt roads of the darkened countryside, hauling wastewater away from well sites. At the time, I was a man haunted by demons of shame and failure. I nursed fresh wounds from a career implosion and the demise of a sixteen-year marriage. The dark, dirty work fit my outlook on life. When I wasn't at work, I'd sit at home, filling and refilling my glass with Jim Beam, staring at the three diplomas of religious master's degrees hanging on the wall, mocking me. Yet I was the one mastered. Mastered by my own destructive faults. So God sent me Willy, unlikely prophet of the oil field.

Willy was a runt of a man who always wore cowboy boots and forgot to put his dentures in about half the time. His had not been an easy life. Hard work and health issues had left their mark on him. He'd been laid off from his most recent job, so now he drove an hour and a half to get to work. Three hours round trip, plus twelve hours on the clock, didn't leave much time for sleep. Or fun. Or family.

Late one night a few of us were sitting around in the break room while our trailers were unloading. Cigarette smoke hung in the air. We sipped thick black coffee to stay awake. One driver looked up from the newspaper to comment on the record high lottery winnings that awaited the guy with the lucky numbers. So we began, one by one, to dream aloud of what we would do with the cash if we won. Buy a mansion on a private island, one said. Travel around the globe, another said. The same worn-out answers we always hear when that game is played. All except Willy.

When it was his turn, Willy took a sip of coffee, gazed at some unseen object on the ceiling, and said, "I tell y'all what I'd do. I'd go find me the biggest double-wide trailer I could get, buy me a few acres of my own, and bring all my family to live with me there. I'd take care of them. We could all just be together. Wouldn't have to worry about nothing. If the good Lord blessed me with that kind of money, we could just kinda kick back and enjoy life together. That'd be my dream come true."

Have you ever experienced one of those occasions when somebody says something that nobody remembers but you? Each word is chiseled into the wall of your memory. You can recall the tone of voice, the cadence of the speech, even the look on the speaker's face. As if, in that moment, the irregular-shaped hole in your heart was perfectly filled by speech divinely molded for it. That was me when Willy spoke.

I was grieving the loss of the life I had wanted for myself. But it had been a life revolving around my ego. My aspirations. My achievements. In the end, my ambition proved my undoing. My marriage was crushed. My children suffered the ripping apart of our family. I lost my job and career, most of my friends, and my carefully planned-out future. I was a divorced, deflated, shamed truck driver teetering on the brink of ultimate despair.

So God paid me a visit. He didn't appear as a clerical collar–wearing, Bible-quoting pastor. He didn't come with a single ecclesiastical credential. God showed up wearing cowboy boots, smoking a cigarette, and dreaming of a simple life full of contentment while surrounded by the family he loved. In Willy's words I heard the voice of the Almighty whispering words of wisdom to a foolish man who had squandered everything. And I heard him calling me back to a life rooted in the beauty of simplicity.

All of us lose our way at one point or another in life. We forget basic, beautiful gifts like family and friends. We chase after phantom pleasures or hollow dreams that will never satisfy our deepest human needs of love and joy. Far too often, in the end, we're left with an even greater emptiness than when we began the pursuit. So God, in mercy, puts a Willy in our path. He is the unlikely shepherd sent to guide us home. Train your ears to listen for him. Your eyes to see beneath the rough exterior. He or she will be the least likely preacher you've ever seen. An inglorious vessel of glorious, life-saving truth.

In that double-wide trailer, surrounded by his family, my friend Willy would have come into his kingdom. He could do more than spend fifteen hours a day on the road and at work. He could settle down into an unadorned life where first things are kept first. Willy's faith in God was extraordinary for its ordinariness. He trusted in God to take care of him and his family whether he won the lottery or not. If he won, so much the better. If not, he'd keep right on doing what needed to be done to put food on the table. He was a husband, father, grandfather who embodied sacrifice. He had a quiet ambition: to love. To give of himself. To consider others more important than he was. Always to ask himself, *What can I do for somebody else, especially my family?*

I worked with Willy for about two years. He never won the lottery, but I struck it rich. I found a holy man in the oil fields, a Solomonic cowboy whose wise words sunk deep into my soul and eventually bore fruit. He reoriented my life away from the grandeur of self-serving accomplishments to the plain beauty of self-sacrificial love. Inside this religious outsider, I was happily surprised to discover a sage and a saint.

How to Amaze Jesus

There are plenty of occasions in the ministry of Jesus when people were surprised as well. They were *thaumazō*—the Greek verb meaning to marvel, surprise, or amaze. For instance, when our Lord calmed the storm at sea, when he caused the fig tree to wither, and when he outsmarted those seeking to entangle him in his speech, the people around him were surprised. They "marveled" or "were amazed" (Matt. 8:27; 21:20; 22:22). They were *thaumazō* at his power and wisdom.

But only on two occasions was Jesus himself *thaumazō*.[1] And both times his amazement or surprise was directly caused by faith, or the lack thereof.

Early in his ministry, when Jesus returned to his hometown of Nazareth to preach in the synagogue, his former neighbors were scandalized by his messianic claims. According to Luke's account, things escalated quickly. They became so enraged they railroaded Jesus out of town and tried to pitch him off a cliff (4:29). Mark simply says, "He could do no mighty work there, except that he laid his hands on a few sick people and healed them" (6:5). Then he adds that Jesus "marveled because of their unbelief" (v. 6).

Those who had watched Jesus grow up, who knew his family, who were Jews, who were the very definition of religious insiders—they rejected him, even tried to murder him. And Jesus's jaw dropped at their unbelief.

About twenty miles away from Nazareth, on the northern shore of the Sea of Galilee, Jesus was amazed once more, this time for the opposite reason. When he entered the city of Capernaum, a Roman centurion begged Jesus to heal his paralyzed servant. When Christ offered to visit this Gentile's home, the centurion said there was no need to go to so much trouble. Jesus need only "say the word" (Matt. 8:8). His word would do the walking. A few power-packed, authoritative syllables from Jesus would have his servant on his feet again in no time. The centurion bet his servant's life on it. Just as soldiers under his command obeyed his orders, what Jesus commanded would come to pass. If he said, "Let it be," it would be. Jesus, he believed, was a Genesis 1 kind of Lord. When he heard the centurion's confession, Christ *thaumazō*: "He marveled and said to those who followed him, 'Truly, I tell you, with no one in Israel have I found such faith'" (v. 10).

The religious insiders—the Jews, the very people of his hometown—surprised Jesus by their lack of faith.

The religious outsider—the soldier, the Gentile—surprised Jesus by his fullness of faith.

It is no different in the twenty-first century than it was in the first. Trust in Christ defies race, ethnicity, gender, sexual orientation, or any other personal or cultural category in which we tend to pigeonhole people. It also defies membership or nonmembership in a religious community. The Spirit is at work wherever his Word is found. And he is at work to help us see this, to rejoice in it, and to embrace our unlikely brothers and sisters in Christ, whoever and wherever they may be.

The Spirit blows willy-nilly across the vast field of humanity, spreading the seeds of grace into all kinds of soil. And often those seeds fall into the "wrong" places, into hearts we think are inhospitable to the message of Christ. Like the heart of a harlot from Jericho, an oil field worker from Texas, a centurion from Capernaum.

In fact, sometimes those seeds spring from cracks in the asphalt more than from the richly fertilized soil of a church's garden—in places like Moab.

Ruth: The Faithful Outsider

The Moabites wouldn't have celebrated their national birthday with the ancient equivalent of fireworks painting the night sky red, white, and blue. Their genesis was on the outskirts of the scorched earth of Sodom and Gomorrah, where the stench of fire and brimstone still polluted the air. A pair of angels had rescued Lot and his two daughters from the hometown's incineration. These three survivors holed up in a cave in the remote hill country until they could figure out where to go next. Where they "went next" is a dark chapter in biblical history.

On two successive nights, the girls pulled out the liquor, got their dad drunk, and had sex with him. Nine months later, they both bore sons of incest. The older of these two daughters named her son Moab, which means "from [my] father." This boy would grow up to become the patriarch of the Moabites.

A nation conceived in the midnight of a cave, in Sodom's shadow, in drunkenness, by incest is about as unlikely a place to find a friend of God as one can imagine. Yet here, among the Moabites, we meet the woman whose fidelity and love is so famous that some of her words are still engraved on the rings of married couples today.

Her name is Ruth. She was a Gentile, a citizen of Moab, who married into an Israelite family when they migrated into her country to escape a famine in the holy land. Over the course of a decade, their lives were punctuated by a series of funerals. One by one, each of the men in the family died, including Ruth's husband. Three women survived: Naomi, the matriarch, and her two daughters-in-law, Ruth and Orpah. When Naomi decided to return to her homeland, she told these Moabite women to remain among their own people, to remarry, to go back to their old gods, to reboot their lives. She was old. Her losses had made her bitter. And, to top it all off, it seemed Yahweh had singled her out to bear the brunt of his ill will.

Orpah wished Naomi a tearful goodbye and walked away. Ruth stood stock-still, stubborn, the strings of her heart interwoven with Naomi's own. "Do not urge me to leave you or to return from following you," she said. "For where you go I will go, and where you lodge I will lodge. Your people shall be my people, and your God my God. Where you die I will die, and there will I be buried. May the LORD do so to me and more also if anything but death parts me from you" (Ruth 1:16–17).

This daughter of Moab may have traced her lineage back to one of the darkest, most despicable episodes in biblical history, but here she stood in the light, overflowing with love, devoted to family, faith, and a future that Yahweh alone would determine.

That future, as mentioned, was eventually to repatriate to the holy land with Naomi, marry a man of Israel named Boaz, and become the great-grandmother of King David. Matthew includes Ruth in his genealogy of the Messiah (1:5).

Dig far enough into the roots of Jesus's family tree and you'll wind up with Ruth in Edom. Dig even deeper and you'll stand in a cave, outside Sodom, with an intoxicated man and two daughters pregnant with his sons. Yet even in this ungodly place God was at work. He was redeeming a seemingly unredeemable situation. He was laying the groundwork for the salvation of the world from a child of incest, who would father a nation from whom would come Ruth, the friend of and spokeswoman for Yahweh. We see the seed of faith fully blossom from soil far outside the confines of Israel. In her quiet, stubborn voice of fidelity to Naomi and God, we hear the Spirit speak.

The Quiet Voices

There's no shortage of loud voices at the center of the religious establishment. From the Vatican, to celebrity pastors of megachurches, to conservative Christian bloggers, when each one speaks, their words ripple across the globe, borne by the waves of social media. A single tweet can become the contemporary "shot heard round the world." Among Christians, these men and women are household names. We listen to their podcasts, ask them to autograph their books, hear them quoted in sermons. And there's nothing wrong with this. There's often wisdom in their words.

The problem is this: our ears can grow so accustomed to these loud voices that we become deaf to the quiet voices whispering profound wisdom on the fringes. God's friends in the oil fields and convenience stores and soup kitchens of the world. The modern-day Rahabs and Ruths and Roman centurions whom we walk right past without ever considering that on their lips might be greater knowledge of Christ than we'll find in a pulpit.

Paul says there weren't many PhDs in the Corinthian church. Not many "wise according to worldly standards" (1 Cor. 1:26). But God purposely chose what the world considers foolish to shame the wise. They weren't from celebrity families. But, again, God chose what is weak, what is low and despised, to shame the strong. Stretching his argument as far as possible, Paul even says that God chose the "things that are not, to bring to nothing things that are" (v. 28). In other words, Christ was at work in this Roman city precisely where no one would expect him to be. Not among the supposedly wise, strong, and rich, but the nobodies. The unnoticed, the uneducated, the uncared for. God's eyes were locked onto men and women to whom the world was blind.

Most of the time, we are blind to these people today. To see God at work, we need to reorient our vision downward, to the humble, low places. To retrain our ears to the quiet voices, to the blue-collar theologians whom God uses to whisper words of wisdom. These are the folks who are not in our path but beside it. The ones we must turn aside to see. Those on the edges. As Jesus "had no form or majesty that we should look at him, and no beauty that we should desire him," so he still lurks in our world among the common, the unattractive, the simple, the forgotten (Isa. 53:2).

For instance, I heard one of the shortest but most memorable sermons not from a pulpit but from beside a dumpster. I had pulled my semi up behind a convenience store to grab a cup of coffee. As I climbed out of the truck, a woman walked up to me. Her face burned a deep brown. Stained jeans and sockless shoes and weary eyes. "Sir," she said, "I hate to bother you, but can you help me?" Pointing over her shoulder, she said her husband was in the dumpster. They were hungry and he was digging for food. Could I give them anything?

When I came out of the store a few minutes later, she and her husband were standing beside my truck. I handed them the two submarine sandwiches I'd bought inside. The man took them, handed them to his wife, and stretched out his hand. I shook it, feeling the grime and grease of the dumpster on his palm. On his weathered face glowed a gratitude more profound than anything I've ever witnessed. "Thank you, sir," he said, "thank you so much. We don't have hardly nothing. Just got to town a few nights ago. Been sleeping under the bridge over there. But God, he always seems to send people to help us out. Jesus been good to us that way. He always provides." And thanking me again, they walked away, out of my life, but never from my memory and gratitude.

A man who had no address, no car, no savings account, who was about to eat out of a trash can—he told me that "Jesus been good to us that way."

Every time I think of that dumpster sermon, uttered by a homeless prophet, I remind myself that wisdom lurks in the outer places. Rich gratitude among the impoverished and forgotten. Jesus been good to us that way. Yes, he has. And Jesus was good to me in sending that man into my life for a few brief moments. He reminded me that God has friends in low places. In low places profound faith flourishes. And from those low places resounds the voice of God from the lips of his people.

Thank God for pastors, for church leaders, for bestselling Christian authors, for all those in positions of prominence whom Christ uses to proclaim his Good News of salvation for the world. But thank God too for people who have never read a word of Martin Luther or Karl Barth but whose lives are inked through and through with the theology of the cross. They drive tractors, flip burgers, shingle roofs, and, yes, dig through dumpsters. Sometimes they are members of a congregation, sometimes not. Some of them, like Rahab, work as prostitutes or at strip clubs. Some of them, like the centurion, carry rifles and wear fatigues. Others, like my friend Willy, drive a truck and dream of a simple life in a double-wide trailer surrounded by the laughter of grandchildren.

Each of them embodies the earthiness of theology. The same God born in a barn and laid in a feed trough is swaddled in the ordinaries of their unawesome lives. The same God who had nowhere to lay his head sleeps with them under interstate bridges. The same God who was blackballed by the religious highbrows of his day sits and mourns with those who have been broken by the church. The same God who died between two crooks hangs out with cons and ex-cons today. The same God who let a prostitute weep on his feet and dry them with her hair embraces and kisses believing women today who have been entangled in the sex trade. He is the God of the cross who is found where the world doesn't seek him—or, all too often, where the church doesn't expect him to be.

Jesus is there for them, for us, for all people. He is a God of surprises, whose ways shock us into expanding our horizons. The laborers in his vineyard may wear suits and ties, boots and jeans, or leather and tats. But they are all his laborers. Or more precisely, his children. God's family is full of misfits. Always has been, always will be. For our Father's family is founded on grace, not goodness.

Discussion Questions

1.   Read Romans 10:12-15. From whom do we ordinarily hear the Word of God taught and proclaimed? Who else does the Lord use to speak his truth? Who are the religious outsiders and how does God use them also to speak his Word? Discuss some examples.

_____

_____

_____

2.   Read Joshua 2:1-21. Who was Rahab and how did she help the Israelite spies? Discuss her words in verses 9-13. What did she know about God? What does she confess about the Lord in verse 11? How was the Lord using her words and actions?

_____

_____

_____

3.   Read Joshua 6:25 and Matthew 1:5. Where does Rahab fit into the broader history of Israel? How did some prostitutes in Jesus' day respond to him and his ministry (Matthew 21:31-32)? Discuss what this reveals about the Lord's unexpected use of religious outsiders who still bear witness of him today.

_____

_____

_____

4.   What does it mean that "all of Israel's sins began in their ears"? Read Jeremiah 7:23-26. Why is it so vital to listen to the Word of the Lord (Isaiah 55:6-11; Hebrews 4:12)? Discuss how we do, or do not, listen to that Word. How does Paul describe the Word of the Gospel (Rom. 1:16)? What does that Gospel give to us?

_____

_____

_____

5.   What does it mean that "outward attachment to a religious institution is no guarantee of an inward attachment to the God of the cross"? Talk about what this means for the life of the church and formal membership in the church.

_____

_____

_____

6.   How did the Lord use Willy to recalibrate and refocus Chad's life? Have you had any similar experiences where Christ, through the simple testimony of a friend or colleague or stranger, pointed you back to a life rooted in faith, hope, and love?

_____

_____

_____

7.   Review the two occasions when Jesus was "amazed" or "marveled" (Mark 6:1-6 and Matthew 8:5-13). How are these two situations different? Discuss how faith is sometimes found where we least expect it. Where might we see that happening in our world today?

_____

_____

_____

8.   Review the story of Ruth. What was the infamous heritage of Moab (Genesis 19:30-38)? What did Ruth promise Naomi (Ruth 1:16-17) and how is she connected to David and Christ (Ruth 4:17-22; Matthew 1:5)? How does this story reveal the way that God has "friends in low places"?

_____

_____

_____

9.   What other examples from Scripture come to mind when you think of the Lord using an unconventional person or a surprising situation to communicate his will? What does it mean that "God's family is full of misfits"? Discuss how this truth can change the way we interact with, and listen to, others?

_____

_____

_____

Three
Godforsaken Hangouts

The north fork of the Red River dances its way through the hills and flatlands of the north Texas county where I grew up. Cottonwoods, like bashful suitors, admire it from a distance, sneaking their roots through the sandy soil to drink of its life. The tracks of whitetail deer, coyotes, and feral hogs freckle the face of its banks. It's a fickle source of water. I've witnessed it swell with pride as storms whip through and flood the creeks feeding into it. And I've knelt on sand in the middle of it and dug a foot down before my fingers felt moisture beneath its desert veneer.

I spent much of my teenage years along this river. Hunting, hiking, exploring the caves sunk into its surrounding cliffs. It was also here, high above the river, that I discovered my very own thin place.

That's what the Celts called them. They believed that in certain sacred locales, the distance between earth and heaven shrinks to an almost translucent veil. It's a thin place, almost like the magical wardrobe that served as a portal to Narnia. Except in a thin place you don't step into a different world. Your world collides with another world. It's a place that strips you down, reconfigures the architecture of your soul.

If you turn your back on the Red River, wrestle your way through the prickly branches of the wild plum bushes, and crawl on hands and knees up the hillside, you come to a fist-shaped boulder. It looks like an ancient god of the underworld thrust his hand through the surface of the earth in defiance.

Once a week, usually on a Sunday afternoon, I would make a pilgrimage to this rock. Pull my way up its pockmarked surface. Perch atop its crown. Gaze at the vista of water and trees and undulating hills fading into the distance. Here I would talk to God. I would dream aloud. I would feel an intimacy with what is unseen.

At the time, I was a child. I spoke like a child. I thought like a child. I reasoned like a child. In order to bask in the presence of the Almighty, I left ordinary life behind. I found a location where I felt the nearness of divinity, where solemnity and sanctity were palpable.

I had no idea that in the future odysseys of my life, I would find that God's chosen hangouts are not necessarily cathedrals of nature. As a boy I sensed God atop that high and grand boulder. As a man I discovered God where God seemed not to be: in the low and obscure crevices of the world.

The Underside of Creation

Jesus says that when he comes again, he will sit on his glorious throne, gather all the nations before him, and separate them as a shepherd separates the sheep from the goats (Matt. 25:31–46). He will address each of the groups, welcoming the believers into the kingdom prepared for them from the foundation of the world and banishing the unbelievers into the eternal fire prepared for the devil and his angels.

This judgment scene is familiar to most Bible readers. What we often skim over, however, is a profound truth embedded in these verses.

To the sheep, Jesus says, "I was hungry and you gave me food, I was thirsty and you gave me drink, I was a stranger and you welcomed me, I was naked and you clothed me, I was sick and you visited me, I was in prison and you came to me" (vv. 35–36). The believers, however, are confused. When did we ever see you hungry or thirsty or otherwise in need? they ask. And Jesus responds, "Truly, I say to you, as you did it to one of the least of these my brothers, you did it to me" (v. 40). In the words of Robert Capon, "The criterion for the rewarding of the sheep is nothing other than their blind acceptance by faith of a king who has appeared to the world only under the guise of the last, the lost, the least, and the little." Jesus was there all along, paradoxically present "on the underside of creation."[1]

We come face-to-face with the Creator on the underside of creation. God wraps around him the mantle of the ungodlike. "For though the LORD is high, he regards the lowly" (Ps. 138:6). Though he is powerful, he dwells among the powerless. When you step into God's personal space, you won't spy a white-bearded old man glowing like fire atop a gilded throne. He looks like a school cafeteria full of third graders. He looks like your nephew who got caught dealing pot and ended up in the county jail. He looks like that guy from accounting who was put in the ICU over the weekend. Wherever the last, the lost, the least, and the little are, that's where God hangs out.

If there truly are thin places in this world, they are thick with the everyday needs of the world.

The Sound of a Low Whisper

There certainly have been moments in history when the Lord manifested himself to people in earth-shaking, awe-inspiring ways. When no eye or ear could miss that they stood on holy ground.

God appeared to Israel when they were camped at Mount Sinai. "There were thunders and lightning and a thick cloud on the mountain and a very loud trumpet blast, so that all the people in the camp trembled" (Exod. 19:16). Sinai was "wrapped in smoke because the LORD had descended on it in fire" (v. 18). These divine pyrotechnics made Israel, and even Moses, cower in fear. This was unmistakably sacred space.

God appeared to Isaiah when he was worshiping in Jerusalem. He saw Yahweh "sitting upon a throne, high and lifted up; and the train of his robe filled the temple" (Isa. 6:1). Six-winged seraphim flew about him, chanting, "Holy, holy, holy is the LORD of hosts; the whole earth is full of his glory!" (v. 3). As the temple shook and the house filled with smoke, Isaiah cried out that he was a dead man. He was unclean yet had laid eyes on the King. Only after an angel purified his lips with a coal from the altar did the prophet regain some composure. Here, too, was clearly holy ground.

These theophanies, or "God-appearances," and others like them in the Old Testament all exhibit a common trait: they left no skeptics, agnostics, or atheists quibbling about what just happened. God crashed humanity's party in a big way. It was a fact as incontrovertible as the sun blazing in the sky. People saw God in his Godness. It was incredible and terrifying. And it was rare.

But the OT appearance that unveils more about God than any other is the one with the smallest wow factor. It too happens at Sinai, but this time Elijah alone is privy to the scene. First, three natural phenomena, all seemingly electrified with divinity, roar past the prophet: a great and strong wind tears mountains apart and breaks rocks in pieces, an earthquake shakes the mount, and tongues of fire lick the earth. Yahweh is rummaging through the loudest costumes in nature's closet. But one by one he leaves them on the hanger. We hear this litany: "But the LORD was not in the wind . . . but the LORD was not in the earthquake . . . but the LORD was not in the fire" (1 Kings 19:11–12).

Then where was he? "After the fire the sound of a low whisper" (v. 12).

The sound of a low whisper. Or "a still small voice," as the King James Version renders it. The Hebrew for "low" or "small" (*dakah*) is used to describe objects that are thin, like the gaunt cows in Pharaoh's dream (Gen. 41:3) or the wafer-like manna (Exod. 16:14). This was not a massive, bellowing sound that reverberated through the wilderness. It was God whispering something under his breath, almost inaudible, easily missed.

The Lord's clothing doesn't fit him. His favorite shirts and pairs of pants are three sizes too small. The flowing wind would have hugged his frame nicely. The earthquake was tailored to his dimensions. The robe of fire was voluminous enough to wrap around his presence. But the voice was all wrong. Too tight. Too confining. It was unbecoming for such a towering divinity to squeeze himself into such a tiny space as a whispering voice.

But he does. That's the point of God's subdued appearance to Elijah. He eschews bigness for littleness. We can walk right past God and never see him, never hear him, never even know he's there. The bells and whistles of Sinai will be absent. We won't spy six-winged seraphim swooshing through the air around us. The space God inhabits will look small and un-divine. A whispering place. It may even look like the last place in the world where you'd expect to take your shoes off because you're treading on sacred soil.

Unseen Altars

The places where we come face-to-face with God are but whispers amid the noise and clamor of our carnival world.

They look like a rocking chair where a mother cradles her crying infant to her breast. Her eyes are heavy, her nerves frazzled. The clock says 2:34 a.m. She's never gone so far on so little sleep. A truck rumbles by outside her home. Moonlight pressing through the window casts strange shadows on the nursery walls. She looks down at the tiny face pressed against her skin, drinking from her body, completely reliant upon her for life. She softly sings the same lullabies her mother once sang to her.

She is a mother. This is her child. And she rocks the chair, back and forth, back and forth, atop an unseen altar. Here, in this place, God is present. He is in her, filling her lungs with air and her breasts with milk. He is in the child, this diapered image of the Creator, knit together in his mother's womb, brought forth as an icon of the Father's love. He is in the feeding and the eating, the giving and the receiving, the profound simplicity of a mother and child doing what they do, being who they are. Here is an altar, a thin place, sacred soil inside a nursery.

These divine appearances look like a John Deere driven by a farmer who pulls a plow to ready the earth for seed. His cap is stained with sweat. His callused hands are the only résumé he has. His father, and his grandfather before him, sank their lives into these acres of west Texas soil. He pours a cup of coffee from a thermos as the tractor crawls along. The last three years were hard on his family. The hail two summers ago. The drought last year. He's got a daughter starting at Tech this fall. So he plows and plants and prays for rain.

He is a farmer. This is his land. And he drives the tractor, back and forth, back and forth, atop an unseen altar. Here, in this place of dirt and fertilizer and seed, God is present. He is in this small-town farmer, cutting arrow-straight furrows through the fields. He is in the plowing and sowing, harvesting and transporting. The diesel fumes rise like incense before the Father's throne. This man is a rural priest, at work in the tabernacle of the farm, raising food to feed a hungry world. Here is another altar, another thin place, more sacred soil.

These divine appearances look like a taxi, honking and weaving its way through the labyrinth of New York City traffic. They look like an outpost in Afghanistan, where a Marine holds a rifle in his hands and dreams of holding his three-year-old daughter again. And they look like lumber mills and coal mines and auto factories, where workers do their jobs, earn their pay, care for their families. These places are thick with the everyday needs of the world. God moves with these believers, back and forth, back and forth, atop the unseen altars of the world, whispering amid the noise, *I am here with you. Your work is sacred. This is how I care for the world, through you, in you, by you.*

These divine appearances also look like a one-bedroom apartment in Cincinnati, Ohio, where a thirty-six-year-old man was curled up in the fetal position in the middle of the floor, holding the barrel of a .357 revolver inside his mouth. Two months earlier, his wife left with their son and daughter to move across the country. He had lost his job, his career, his friends, and his reputation. Now he had lost his family. There was nothing to live for. So he drained the bottle of Jim Beam. Picked up his pistol. Crumbled onto the middle of the floor. And his finger hovered over the trigger of eternity.

That man was me, twelve years ago. I rocked my body, back and forth, back and forth, atop an unseen altar. Here, in this place of tears and regret and hopelessness, God was present. He was in this broken man, pulling him back from the brink of death. He hunkered down in the darkness with me. The Spirit prayed within me with groans too deep for words. In this place where God seemed a million miles away, he was as close as the blood dripping from my fragmented heart. Here God erected an altar over the chasm of despair. Here was a thin place thick with suffering. Here was sacred soil soaked with the tears of a failed, fallen, yet forgiven child of God.

God's holy places often look like godforsaken places. Like the floor of a one-bedroom apartment. Like a divorce court. Like a rehab. Like a 2½ x 8 foot hole in the ground about to swallow the body of your husband, your mom, your twelve-year-old son. And you cry, "O God, why? Where the hell are you when I need you? Why have you forsaken me?" In the deepest crevices of depression, grief, and loss, when our eyes look up and all we see is the closed door of heaven, slammed in our face—there, too, is sacred space.

These darkest times of our lives are the wilderness years. Our Father takes us where we don't want to go, where we are stripped of control, where we sit with Moses, Israel, David, Elijah, and Jesus in desert sands. There we learn our whole lives hang solely on the Word of our God.

The Nothing Years

The four decades that the people of God spent in the wilderness were the best and the worst years of Israel's history.

They were the worst because it was a "great and terrifying wilderness, with its fiery serpents and scorpions and thirsty ground where there was no water" (Deut. 8:15). It was the un-Eden, where everything wrong with the world seemed to be on steroids. There was no food, no water, no protection from the elements, no fortress from foes, nothing but death dogging their steps day after day. It appeared like the last place in the world they would encounter the God of life.

And they were the best years of Israel's history because, in this godforsaken place, God did not forsake them. He moved in with them. He traveled with them. He suffered with them. When they were hungry, Yahweh served up manna from heaven's kitchen. When they were thirsty, he transformed a rock of flint into a fountain of water. Their clothes never got threadbare and their sandals never wore out (29:5). Where there was nothing, God provided everything.

In Israel's decades of wandering through the desert sands, Yahweh was humbling, testing, and disciplining them, as a father does his son (8:2–4). He knocked away every support they had. He stripped them of all their resources. He reduced them to nothing. They became the ideal material for God to use.

As he created all things from nothing, solely by the power of his Word, so his ongoing creative work in the world remains unaltered. From the nothing of weakness, he creates strength. From the nothing of hunger, he creates manna. From the nothing of vulnerability, he creates protection. In every wilderness experience, God is pounding away at a singular lesson: "man does not live by bread alone, but man lives by every word that comes from the mouth of LORD" (v. 3).

Amid the storm of other voices that predict our doom comes the sound of a low whisper from the mouth of the Lord: *Fear not. I am with you. I will never leave you nor forsake you. You are my beloved child in Jesus Christ.*

That is the everything-voice that speaks hope into the nothing-years of our lives. We don't orchestrate these years in the wilderness. We don't daydream of being shipped out into the desert of tears or divorce or mourning. These things show up on our doorstep uninvited. They take us by the arm and force us away from our homes, our white picket fences, our safe and comfortable existence, into a nightmare come true. Into a great and terrifying wilderness. Into the arms of death itself. They are the worst of years, not only because we lose all our safety nets but because it feels like we're in a place that is off-limits even to God.

Almost everyone I know who has lived in their own wilderness will admit that, though they would never opt to revisit that place, it was there they learned the most about the nearness of God. Tikhon Shevkunov, for instance, in his book *Everyday Saints and Other Stories*, recounts the story of a Russian Christian named Gabriel who learned this lesson.[2] This man had a glowing résumé: he had founded churches in eastern Russia, served a mission in Jerusalem, and been abbot of a monastery. But along the way, his infamous temper derailed his ministry. In a heated confrontation with a priest, he had tossed the man out of his church and down a flight of stairs.

In a disciplinary action, he was forbidden to serve in the Orthodox clergy for three years. He left town in disgrace. Soon his meager savings had dried up. When he could find no other means to earn a living, he took a job as a groundskeeper. He who once was surrounded by splendor and power now spent his days in the dirt, on his knees, weeding gardens.

In later years, when he had been restored to the ministry and even elevated to a bishop, he was asked, "What was the happiest time of your life?" He thought for a while and responded, "The very happiest times of my life were the years when I was suspended and disgraced. Never before or since in my life was the Lord as close to me as back then."[3] Gabriel's sense of the nearness of Christ was never greater than when he was working as a common laborer in his own wilderness.

Like Gabriel, many of us discover in the nothing years that nothing will separate us from the love of God in Jesus Christ. We find in this place thick with suffering yet one more thin place where Christ is but a breath away.

The worst years turn out to be the years in which Jesus does his best work within us. It is in the wilderness that we learn to live solely by the Word that comes from the mouth of our Savior.

Hope in the Parking Lot

Not only does the Lord sustain us by his Word in our own nothing years but he also uses our lips to speak words of grace to those trapped in their own wilderness. He places in our path the last, the lost, the least, and the little. In our giving to them, and in their receiving of the Lord's gifts, we encounter God in disguise. He's hidden in places we didn't expect him to be. Places like a Kroger's parking lot.

About four years ago a young woman named Cindy was sitting alone outside a grocery store. Though surrounded by cars and asphalt and all the trappings of city life, she was just as isolated as if she were exiled into Sinai's desert sands. Her face was a map of her soul, with oceans of tears and continents of emotions. She had never felt so utterly banished from hope. She had very little money. She was stranded. Her boyfriend had turned his back on her. Walked out of her life. And in two days Cindy was scheduled to visit an abortion clinic to do what she didn't want to do but had decided was her only choice.

There happened to be another young woman in the parking lot that day. A friend of mine named Michelle. She was twenty-one years old. A university student. Michelle was not a woman on a mission. She was not actively seeking out someone she could help. She was simply going about her daily routine, ticking items off her to-do list. She needed some groceries for the fridge. So she pulled into Kroger's, parked her car, and began working her way toward the store.

And in the middle of that sea of asphalt she bumped her shin on one of God's hidden altars of grace.

Michelle noticed the young woman weeping. Neither one knew the other. Cindy was simply a stranger in need, thirsting for the water of compassion. So Michelle came to her. Knelt down. Asked if there was anything she could do to help. Over the next fifteen minutes the only help she could give was simply to be there. Not to leave. Cindy wept. She couldn't speak. So Michelle waited. Rubbed her shoulder. And soon these two strangers, unexpectedly united by grief, began to cry together.

Finally Cindy's tears gave way to words. She began to tell her story. The abandonment. The desperation. The pregnancy. The planned abortion. Michelle listened. Whatever other plans she had that day were no longer important. She had stumbled upon a thin place where heaven and earth touched. When this young, unmarried, pregnant woman felt utterly alone, forsaken by all, without a hope in the world, Jesus appeared. He was in Cindy's need and he was in Michelle's love. Together they wept and talked over an invisible altar where the crucified and risen king of grace was enthroned.

A few months later, in a hospital room, Cindy smiled down at the face of her newborn baby swaddled in a pink blanket. Cindy's encounter with Michelle that day, and the friendship that blossomed from it, had been a turning point in her life. A resurrection. When she felt that her life was over, God spoke life into her through the lips of a stranger.

In the parking lot that day, Michelle had told Cindy about a pregnancy center that provided resources to women in need. She told her that she knew it was scary but that both she and the child could make it. There was hope, there was a future for both of them, there was a God who loved them both. Cindy said that she'd never met someone who cared as much as Michelle. She described her friend as a "woman of faith."

Indeed, she is. Both women are. They are bound together by a common trust in the Lord who doesn't forsake us in godforsaken places. He is there, as the psalmist says, collecting our tears in his bottle of remembrance (Ps. 56:8). He is with us in the low and unawesome crevices of the world. And he leads us to those same crevices where, quite unexpectedly, we find others trapped. Family, friends, coworkers, and complete strangers. They are all children of God, masks of Jesus. They are people like Cindy, for whom a listening ear and loving words mean the difference between life and death, hope and despair.

Michelle drove to the store that day to buy some groceries. She didn't realize that the Spirit was guiding her on a pilgrimage, that she was about to step onto holy ground. For in God's ordering of our lives and of the world, an altar can look like black asphalt baptized with tears.

Casserole Pilgrimage

Pilgrimages, journeys to a sacred place, are a central feature of most religions. One of the five pillars of Islam is the Hajj, the pilgrimage to Mecca. Muslims travel to this city from all over the globe to worship at the holiest site of their religion. Hindus visit the city of Varanasi, famous as the spiritual capital of India. Pilgrims walk down the *ghats*, the steps descending into the Ganges River. In these waters, sacred to Hindus, funeral rites are performed and worshipers bathe their bodies. Jews and Christians often journey to the holy city of Jerusalem, to stand on the very soil where so much of their respective histories took shape. Here the temple, the heart of ancient Judaism, once stood. And in this sacred place, the Christian pilgrim can visit the traditional locations associated with the life and ministry of Jesus.

GODFORSAKEN HANGOUTS

To embark on such a pilgrimage as a Christian, you leave behind your home, your job, your neighbors, your responsibilities. You temporarily cut ties with all the ordinary stuff of daily life. You cross over into an extraordinary sphere imbued with sacred significance. If you travel to Jerusalem, you walk the *Via Dolorosa*, the Way of Sorrows, tracing the footsteps of Jesus down the street where he carried his cross. You step into the Church of the Holy Sepulchre, which enshrines both the place of Jesus's crucifixion and the tomb where his body lay. Perhaps you drive a few miles south to Bethlehem to see the Grotto of the Nativity, where the Christ child lay.

I haven't visited the Holy Land. I hope to someday. People who have made this pilgrimage tell me it's a once in a lifetime experience. That it's incredible to be in the same place Jesus was. To soak in the sights and sounds and smells of the ancient metropolis. One friend told me his tour made the Bible seem "more real." Another told me it left him forever changed. It was, in his words, "beyond awesome."

As interesting and even life-changing as such pilgrimages might be, there is a danger associated with them. The message they convey can undermine the message that Jesus himself preached. The impression is given that if you desire to visit a sacred site, if you want to be in the real place where Jesus was, you need to obtain your passport, board a plane, and fly halfway across the world to reach it. To be in a truly thin place, kneel before the Grotto of the Nativity or walk through the doors of the Church of the Holy Sepulchre.

Yet there is another way. Walk through your neighbor's door, carrying a casserole in your arms and love in your heart to comfort her upon the death of her husband. Pray with her, weep with her, share Jesus's presence in his words of life and resurrection. Bring the soil of Jerusalem into her family room. Because that, too, is a Christian pilgrimage. That, too, is the real place where Jesus is.

To visit the site where Jesus was crucified, you need only spend some time with those who bear the crosses of sickness, loss, grief, loneliness, persecution. Golgotha is as close as the nearest hospital. It's down the street at the Starbucks where you meet a friend who got laid off work six months ago and is fighting the demons of depression. The cross is where Jesus is—for though resurrected, he is always the crucified Christ. In, with, and under the crosses of his children is the cross of Jesus himself. They are crucified with him. And their crosses are grafted as branches onto the tree of his cross. Calvary is as close as the nearest person in need of grace and mercy.

The places where Jesus did his most extraordinary work were ordinary places. The underside of creation. A boat floating in the water where he taught the crowds gathered on the shore. A house where Peter's mother-in-law lay sick in bed. An upper room where he washed the feet of his disciples and shared one final meal with them. And a patch of ground outside the city where criminals were nailed to beams of wood, displayed for mockery by onlookers, and forced to endure an agonizing death.

The thinnest place in the history of the world was where all the glory of the almighty God was shrouded beneath nails and thorns and wrapped in the skin of a dying man. The Son of God lamented, "My God, my God, why have you forsaken me?" (Matt. 27:46). And in that still, small voice of our crucified Savior we hear the certainty that God will never forsake us.

In my childhood, as I sat atop that rock overlooking the Red River, I dreamed of great things I could do in the service of God. I prayed that he would use me in powerful ways. I would stay there, anchored to the stone as the afternoon sun began its slow descent. I didn't want to leave this place where I felt enveloped by the aura of the holy.

Three decades have now passed. During those thirty years Christ has enrolled me in the school of the cross. He has revealed to me that it's not our calling to do great things in his service. He doesn't need us to pull off Olympic performances in the kingdom of God. Nor does he desire that we climb rocks to stand in his presence. If he leads us anywhere, it's downward. Not to mountaintops but valleys. Not into cathedrals of nature but into the squalor of a world littered with wrecked lives in need of mercy.

The needle in the Spirit's compass that directs us to where God is always points south. Downward. We descend into his presence. Where the lowly are, there he is. Where the common duties of life are performed, he is at work. If you want to discover the presence of God, don't leave your wife behind for a week of deep meditation in the Rocky Mountains. Go help her do the dishes. If you want to be where Jesus really is, there's no need to kneel before the Grotto of the Nativity. Go change your child's dirty diaper.

Where God is most acutely present he will seem most profoundly absent. He doesn't play by our rules. He doesn't conform to our expectations. Rather he transforms our minds and enlightens our eyes so that we might see him where he is unseeable. In thin places thick with suffering, sweat, tears, and common duties like washing dishes and changing diapers, he will be present. He is most at home where he is most hidden.

Discussion Questions

1. Read Matthew 25:31-46. Where does Jesus tell the two groups of people that he has hidden himself? Discuss the quote from Robert Capon, "The criterion for the rewarding of the sheep is nothing other than their blind acceptance by faith of a king who has appeared to the world only under the guise of the last, the lost, the least, and the little." How is Jesus present "on the underside of creation"?

    _____

    _____

    _____

2. Read Psalm 138:6 and Luke 1:52-53. Why does the Scripture place so much emphasis on God looking toward the lowly, the humble, the downtrodden, the small and weak? Why are we so much more inclined to look up to the powerful and rich and famous? Discuss these words: "If there truly are thin places in this world, they are thick with the everyday needs of the world."

    _____

    _____

    _____

3. Review the theophanies or God-appearances in Exodus 19:18-19, Isaiah 6:1-1, and 1 Kings 19:1-18. How does the Lord's appearance to Elijah differ from the first two? Discuss what is meant by the "still, small voice" and how that reveals a divine preference for subdued appearances, for littleness over bigness. What does that look like today?

    _____

    _____

    _____

4. Go over the examples of "unseen altars." What other instances would fit this same description? Read Isaiah 45:15. How does God hide himself? In what kinds of situations, people, or events is Christ hidden?

    _____

    _____

    _____

5.   How does Deuteronomy 8:15 describe the wilderness? The people of God spent forty years in that wilderness. What was he teaching his people? How does this connect to the forty days that Jesus spent in the wilderness (Matthew 4:1-11)?

_____

_____

_____

6.   Talk about Gabriel's comment that "the very happiest times of my life were the years when I was suspended and disgraced." What insights can we derive from his observation? Discuss how our worst years or hardest season in life can also be the time in which Jesus does his best work within us.

_____

_____

_____

7.   What can we learn from the story of Cindy and Michelle? Describe similar situations in your life, or in the lives of others, where a listening ear and loving words made a world of difference. Relate this to Romans 12:15 and 2 Corinthians 1:3-4.

_____

_____

_____

8.   Talk about the section "Casserole Pilgrimage." In what areas of our lives can we make a "pilgrimage" closer to home? Discuss this quote, "The thinnest place in the history of the world was where all the glory of the almighty God was shrouded beneath nails and thorns and wrapped in the skin of a dying man." How does the crucifixion of Jesus ultimately define for us where God can be found?

_____

_____

_____

Four

Unorthodox Headhunter

Some of my earliest memories were made with a saddle between my knees and reins in my hands. My dad, born an equestrian at heart, had me riding a horse before I could ride a bicycle. He also had me filling water troughs and helping dole out alfalfa and oats. I quickly understood that owning horses meant owning the work involved in caring for them too.

Every week, my family would wind down the ruts of a mesquite covered pasture to an arena on the outskirts of Jal, New Mexico. There, with a group of friends, we'd saddle up and rope steers, and the kids would compete in rodeo events like poles and barrels. This was my first playground. And it was also my first place of employment.

I was paid $1 per roper to poke and prod the cattle into the chutes and, when the cowboy nodded his head, to push the lever that released the steer into the arena, the horse hot on his heels. It would have qualified as one of Mike Rowe's "Dirty Jobs." By the end of the night I would be splattered with manure from my boots to my hat. But I loved the work. I loved the animals. And it didn't hurt that my wallet was usually fat with one-dollar bills by the end of the night.

Over the years, like most people, I've tried my hand at various jobs. Farm worker, cowboy, feed store employee, dishwasher, carpenter's assistant, roofer, pastor, professor, and truck driver. Twice I even flew halfway across the globe to serve as lecturer at a small seminary in Novosibirsk, Siberia. Some jobs required more brain, some more brawn, but each of them required of me a certain aptitude for the task at hand. And each of them also pushed me beyond my abilities. Every workplace was also a school of sorts. I might be learning something as elementary as how to operate an industrial dishwasher or as complicated as how best to teach the intricacies of the Hebrew verbal system.

The jobs in my youth also prompted me to ask myself that nagging question: *What do I want to be when I grow up?* Or, as I would often ponder, *What does God want me to do with my life?* I was vague on specifics, but I was certain of one thing: God and I both agreed that I should be "that guy." You know, that guy who has li[fe] figured out. That guy who, through soul-searching and fervent praying, manage[d] riffle through the files in God's head until he found the manila folder containing grand blueprint for his life. That guy who earned the right degrees, hung out the right crowd, married the right woman, and landed not only the right j[ob] the one God had designed just for him. The one that fit his skills, aptitudes, experience, and passions to a tee. That's who I wanted to be when I grew up—that guy.

I eventually discovered, as most of us do, that guy doesn't exist.

What does exist is a life that's more like a labyrinth than a blueprint. We might have a vague idea of what the next few feet look like, but who knows what will be around the corner: Another corner? A dead end? A long stretch that leads us right back to where we started? "God writes straight with crooked lines," the Portuguese proverb says. He certainly does. God is all about crooked lines, labyrinthine odysseys in life, and plenty of long drives that end in cul-de-sacs. While "that guy" is a figment of our optimistic imaginations, real people in real-life situations grow up to be certain of one thing: the uncertainties of life, jobs, careers, and relationships.

And that's a good thing. Uncertainties are one of the most underappreciated gifts in life. If we could get our hands on a copy of our biography, penned by an author with time-travel capabilities, we shouldn't read it. Certainly not the chapters that document our future. For one thing, there's likely to be some dark material in there, which we'd be better off not knowing until the storm actually arrives. "Sufficient unto the day is the evil thereof," as Jesus reminds us (Matt. 6:34 KJV).

More importantly, knowing our futures would ruin what God is doing in our lives right now. He is guiding us down a labyrinth, full of twists and turns and setbacks, in which we learn about ourselves, others, and God. And one of the most important lessons he's teaching us is this: what we deem as our greatest strengths are usually our greatest weaknesses. And what we think are our greatest weaknesses are the raw material God prefers to use to demonstrate his strength. He uses our losses, struggles, and deficiencies—the very aspects of ourselves we associate with failure—as the vehicles for his kind of success in our life.

In other words, he deals with us as he did with Moses.

The Octogenarian Redeemer

There was a time when Moses knew what God wanted him to do with his life. He had it all figured out. He had celebrated his fortieth birthday. Not too young, not too old. He was schooled in the arts and wisdom of the Egyptians. He was bilingual. He could debate politics in the palace with his adoptive family. And he could also converse with his Hebrew brothers as they slaved away in the fields. He straddled two diametrically opposed worlds: he was an insider by adoption and an outsider by birth. He wore a royal robe, but his heart was clothed with the garb of the slaves.

Eventually, Moses came to a crossroads. He had to choose whether he would called the son of Pharaoh's daughter" and "enjoy the fleeting pleasures of sin" e mistreated with the people of God" (Heb. 11:24–25). He made his choice. uld stand with the powerless, with his kindred. He was convinced that God had handpicked him to liberate his people from bondage (Acts 7:25). And he was right—halfway at least.

He was right about the calling, but he was dead wrong about the timing.

Moses assumed that if there were ever a time to make a move, it was now. The iron was hot. Time to strike. Perhaps he could use his political sway to stage a coup. Or maybe he could secretly mobilize the slaves in a rebellion. He would devise a plan. If nothing else, he could use his muscle to alleviate the sufferings of individual Israelites. Word would get around that they had an ally in the palace, that Moses had not forgotten his roots.

One day the opportunity presented itself. When Moses saw an Egyptian beating up a Hebrew slave, he in turn struck the Egyptian, killing him. No turning back now. He'd drawn first blood. Burying the body in a shallow grave, he walked away as if nothing had happened. The next day, he came upon another fight, only this time two Hebrews were having it out with each other. He stepped between them and said, "Why do you strike your companion?" One of the men responded, "Who made you a prince and a judge over us? Do you mean to kill me as you killed the Egyptian?" (Exod. 2:13–14).

Clearly, this was not the response Moses had hoped for. Didn't this brother realize God was using Moses to save Israel? Rejection threw a monkey wrench into his plans. On top of that, he had not expected that word of his murderous act would spread so quickly. What if someone informed the Egyptian police, or if Pharaoh himself found out? Soon Moses's worst fears were realized. An arrest warrant was issued. Moses was wanted, dead or alive. Preferably dead.

So this man who had God's plan for his life all figured out, this would-be redeemer, tucked his tail between his legs, ran away from everything and everyone he'd ever known, and went on the lam for the next four decades in the desert sands of the Sinai peninsula.

Moses thought he was ready, but God knew better. He needed to be unreadied. To be weakened. To be whittled down. To watch the sands slowly fall in the hourglass of the Sinai. The Lord subjected him to a prolonged crucifixion, a gradual putting to death of every advantage, every strength, he had in Egypt. The desert was his Golgotha. Here the royal prince died and rose a simple shepherd. He was crucified to the palace and resurrected to the tent. For forty years God laid a cross on Moses's back. He undid him so he could redo him. He made Moses think he had failed. Nothing would come of his life now. He was just a keeper of his father-in-law's sheep. He would die a forgotten man, decomposing in the desert sands. Ashes to ashes, dust to dust, prince to pauper.

When the Lord finally appeared to him in the burning bush, telling Moses to return to Egypt on a mission of redemption, the hot zeal of this would-be savior had grown ice cold. He went round and round with Yahweh. He trotted out every excuse he could dream up. No, he was not the man for the job. He was an octogenarian now. He didn't even know God's name. God could just pick someone else, thank you very much. Someone more quick-tongued, more persuasive, with greater faith, without a price on his head back home. In other words, send someone like Moses was decades earlier, before his life of strength and privilege had crumbled around him.

But God, in his undoing of Moses, knew exactly what he was doing. He was wielding the losses, struggles, and deficiencies of this man as vehicles for divine success. He was transforming him, outwardly, into the wrong man for the job. But as Nadia Bolz-Weber points out, "Sometimes the fact that there is nothing about you that makes you the right person to do something is exactly what God is looking for."[1]

If God had contracted a headhunter to find a redeemer for his people, he wouldn't have given the application of Moses more than a passing glance. He certainly wouldn't have flown him in for an interview.

But in God's eyes, because Moses was all wrong, he was all right. The Lord would use Moses's weaknesses to showcase his strength. He would shine his light through the cracks in this broken vessel. As at Golgotha, where the Lord hid his glory beneath a dying man, so in Moses the concealed glory of Yahweh would be manifest.

God would manifest his glory secretly, in an inglorious way, for it would shine through the man Scripture describes as the most meek or humble man on the face of the earth (Num. 12:3). Not a chest-thumping autocrat. Not a bombastic blowhard. But a man bowed low by suffering, shaped by the cruciform hand of God, to be the blessedly wrong man for the right job of serving as a secret agent of Israel's King.

Secret Agents

Old Testament scholar John Kleinig describes Christians as secret agents in this world. It's a fitting description. We have dual citizenship. "We are, in every way, citizens of this world, with earthly homes and earthly jobs and earthly identities," Kleinig writes. In that way, we are no different than our Muslim coworker or the agnostic mechanic who changes our car's oil. We lead ordinary lives surrounded by ordinary people. "Yet at the same time," he continues, "we are citizens of heaven, extraordinary people, aliens working to promote God's gracious rule here on earth. Behind the front of our ordinary lives, we work as secret agents of the heavenly King." We have "a holy secret vocation as members of His royal priesthood."[2]

Like Moses in the desert, we lead ordinary, outwardly unpriestly lives. He was a simple shepherd, armed only with a wooden staff. We aren't identifiable by special clothing, secret handshakes, or telltale jewelry like a cross around our neck. What we do wear—everywhere we go, whatever we do—is the righteousness of Jesus. We wear God's dazzlingly white clothing, laundered at the cross in the bleaching blood of Jesus. Our bodies are the temple of his Spirit. Our lips are the mouthpiece of his Word. Our hands are his hands, our feet his feet. In other words, Jesus, our great high priest, inhabits the humble abode of our lives to do labor in this world, as he did through Moses. In and through us, his clandestine agents, he is slowly advancing his kingdom of grace.

You'd never know it from looking at us. That's why we're secret agents. Secret not in the sense of stealthy or underhanded but as bearing no resemblance to what the world reckons as sacred or God-worthy. As a feed trough was not a worthy crib for the Christ, as prostitutes and tax collectors were not his worthy dinner guests, and as a bloody cross was not a worthy throne, so the ways and means of God's priests in this world are shrouded by that which seems beneath such a grand deity. While the world anticipates God to locate himself in power, wealth, or anything dubbed glorious and attractive in their eyes, he is ensconced in the exact opposite. His secret agents command no one's attention. We realize our profound weaknesses. We see in the mirror a spiderweb of flaws splayed out across our lives. We are just as racked by sin as any unbeliever.

But that's no problem. So we wrestle with weaknesses. So our closets have enough skeletons to populate a graveyard. So we weren't voted Most Likely to Succeed or marched home from Sunday school with ribbons for Bible memorization. Our virtues are not our confidence, nor our vices our doubts. This is not about us. Neither how good we think we are or how bad we know we are constitute our identity or empower us for the missions on which God sends us. "Cursed is the man who trusts in man and makes flesh his strength," Jeremiah says, but "blessed is the man who trusts in the LORD, whose trust is the LORD" (Jer. 17:5, 7). Our trust is in Christ, whose cross and identity we share. "I have been crucified with Christ. It is no longer I who live, but Christ who lives in me" (Gal. 2:20). Our crucified King chooses the last and the least over the first and the greatest. He makes it clear that it is not by human wherewithal but by divine grace that his agents operate in this world.

As if to prove this to us, once and for all, God decided to put forward the most extreme and comical example he could come up with. He sent a holier-than-thou xenophobic bigot to preach to a group of godless, infamous terrorists. Talk about mission impossible. Talk about choosing the wrong man for the job. But if there's ever been a narrative confirming that the Lord upends our expectations, that he alone is at work in his secret agents to get the job done, it's this one. It's the story of Jonah and Nineveh.

The Hawkish Prophet

Jonah's name in Hebrew means "dove," but he had the personality of a hawk. Ready to swoop down on the prey. Talons eager to rip flesh. Thirsty for blood. Assyrian blood, to be exact. They were Public Enemy #1 in ancient Israel. They skinned their enemies, impaled them, and left them out in the open to be picked apart by scavengers. These people behaved like animals. They were hated and feared. A nation that fine-tuned the perverse art of terror.

And they were Jonah's mission field.

"Go to Nineveh," the capital of Assyria, "and call out against it," God told Jonah (Jon. 1:2). The prophet responded by letting his feet do the talking. He stomped off in the opposite direction, bound for Tarshish. There's a telling digression as the story unfolds: Jonah gradually moves "down." Down to the seaside town of Joppa, down into a ship, down into the inner part of the ship, down into the sea, and finally down into the belly of the fish. He's falling from his pinnacle of pride, plummeting into death itself. Why? Because often it's only in our self-dug graves that we discover Easter. Jonah did. In the guts of a fish, this hawkish man mourns like a dove. He prays for mercy. And receives it.

Vomited ashore by the fish, he travels to Nineveh. Spends three days preaching. And by the end of the third day, he's not been skinned alive, impaled, or even roughed up. The unimaginable transpires. These terror-loving people sit on the edge of their seats as he speaks. They fall all over themselves repenting. In a move without precedent in the Bible, they even clothe their cows in sackcloth and force them to fast alongside them. These sinners are serious about repentance. They hear, they believe, they pray for clemency. "Who knows?" they say. "God may relent and turn from his fierce anger" (see 3:10). A confession not exactly sparkling with confidence, but it does bear fruit. God sees and relents. The city is spared.

And Jonah? He just wants to die. His dovelike humility vanishes and his hawkish pride wings its way to the surface once more. Hatred crawls all over him. Finally, in an epic temper tantrum, he tells us why he ran away from his calling to begin with. "O LORD," he says, "is not this what I said when I was yet in my country? That is why I made haste to flee to Tarshish; for I knew that you are a gracious God and merciful, slow to anger and abounding in steadfast love, and relenting from disaster" (4:2). You can almost hear him spitting out every snarky word.

Jonah was angry at God for being God. He didn't want to preach because he feared the worst: that the heart of God would be revealed to Nineveh, that these evil people wouldn't get their comeuppance. Jonah's nightmare was that his mission impossible would be mission success. Unwilling to live in a world in which grace is victorious, the prophet requests that the Almighty just put him out of his misery. Better to die than to watch his enemies live in the joy of the absolution.

The book of Jonah ends with the prophet sulking on the outskirts of the city, with God posing a rhetorical question to him, "Should I not pity Nineveh . . . ?" (v. 11). What kind of God would I be, he inquires, if I showed no mercy? I would not be true to myself, that's for sure. I would be the kind of God the world really wants and expects. I would be a tit-for-tat deity who operates like Santa, giving gifts to good little boys and girls, and nothing to the bad ones, except maybe a coal in their stocking.

That's the God we easily believe in because that's how things work in our world. If Nineveh was that evil, they deserved a drone strike, not a preacher of forgiveness. If people are wicked and they get punished, well, that's what they had coming.

But because the Lord is "a gracious God and merciful, slow to anger and abounding in steadfast love, and relenting from disaster" (v. 2), he gave them what they didn't have coming. He gave them his heart. The same heart displayed at Calvary. The heart that beats to the rhythm of his love for us. The heart that takes no pleasure in the death of the wicked but delights in—and effects—our repentance and restoration.

And God does all this, in the case of Nineveh, through a secret agent who dragged his feet, who despised his congregation, and who wanted nothing more than for God to nuke the entire city. If you feel the need to laugh, go right ahead. The scene is so preposterous it's hard to keep a straight face. This is part of the sacred humor of God. Jonah is the punch line. And the joke's message is this: God's work is not about us. It's about him and him alone.

Divine strength only fits inside weak vessels. Jonah was too big for God to fit inside him. So God shrunk him in the sea, in the fish, in the "failure," so he could squeeze into him. The bigger we are, the more engorged our egos, the less of God will fit inside us. He is the God of small spaces. He is "near to the brokenhearted," says the psalmist, for the tiny shards of a shattered heart are just the right size for him to fit inside (Ps. 34:18).

If the Lord had sent a willing preacher to Nineveh, one who graduated with honors from a prophetic seminary, who had a keen cultural admiration for the Ninevites, then we would be all the poorer for it. We'd not have this story of Jonah. We'd not have as clear a sense of how radically counterintuitive God's work is. He uses failures for success, fools for a wise man's errand, that we might grasp how he will accomplish our salvation in his Son, and through that Son continue to work in our lives as well.

He works by writing his story over our story.

God's Story inside Our Stories

Dual narratives are unfolding in our lives at every moment. There's the story we're writing, and the one penned by the Spirit. A great deal of overlap exists between these two narratives, but there's plenty of divergence as well.

The story we're writing goes something like this. We live our lives in the freedom God has given to us. We fall in love, get married, raise a family. Or we remain single, foster friendships, cultivate hobbies. We go to school, find a career, purchase a home. We discover what makes us tick, where our passions lie, then try to find activities and responsibilities that match those. We settle into our place in this world. Life may not be perfect, but it's good, or at least okay. We plan where we'll be this coming Christmas with the full certainty that it will happen. We decide where our kids will go to school. How we'll celebrate our fifth or twenty-fifth wedding anniversary. So our story unfolds.

And then there's God's story. His narrative is writ large when ours shrinks under pressure. When ours is in eight-point font, his is in all caps. Our marriage becomes strained, or we divorce, or our teenage daughter tells us she's pregnant. This is not the story we want written. The company where we've worked for the last ten years goes belly-up and we're forced into a new career. We spend the weekend visiting pawn shops to find the tools or jewelry our son hocked to pay his dealer for a fix. This is not the narrative we had planned. This is not a life we forecast or one we can control. We don't have the emotional resources to deal with it. Everything we didn't want to happen has happened.

But this is God's story happening inside our story. His own narrative is superimposed over our own. And he's an eccentric author. We write our story in a way that draws upon our strengths, our hopes, our plans and dreams. But he writes our story in a way that highlights our weaknesses, our fears, our deficiencies. Why? Because in so doing he showcases the areas of our lives where he does his best work. Yes, of course, he can and does use our unique talents and abilities, but most often he uses whatever is going to spotlight our nothingness and his everything.

His story in our lives is most obvious when the narrative has taken a turn toward the cross.

"When I am weak, then I am strong," said the apostle Paul (2 Cor. 12:10). But this confession only comes after complaint. He pleaded, three times, for the Lord to extract his "thorn in the flesh" (v. 7). Paul had his story to write, after all, and the Lord's thorn was getting in the way of his narrative. But God dug in his heels. No, the thorn stays, he said. "My grace is sufficient for you, for my power is made perfect in weakness" (v. 9). In other words, if Paul is powerful, Jesus is weak in him. If Paul is weak, Jesus is powerful in him. The more Paul gets to write his own story, the less the story of Jesus gets told. So the apostle, finally realizing this, says, "Therefore I will boast all the more gladly of my weaknesses, so that the power of Christ may rest upon me. For the sake of Christ, then, I am content with weaknesses, insults, hardships, persecutions, and calamities. For when I am weak, then I am strong" (vv. 9–10).

The stories we prefer to write about ourselves, as outwardly attractive as they may be, will never get us into the narrative in which Christ truly shapes us into his own image. The self-image we cultivate tends to work on the false assumption that God desires us to grow more independent. To become better and stronger so that we need him less. We imagine ourselves growing when we lean less on God and more on our own gifts and talents. As if the Lord is waiting for us to spread our wings and make our own way through this life.

But Christian maturity is not marked by independence but dependence. A growing awareness of our incessant need for Christ. A focus off me, my talents, my doing, even my religious life, and a focus instead upon the Son of God. The less we are, the more Christ is. But far from being bad news, this is the best news of all. For the more Christ is, the more we are the very people God has created us to be.

God's narrative is always written with the ink of the cross. He's trying to get it through our thick heads that his kingdom is a backward place where last is first, least is greatest, dead is alive. His narratives include thorns in the flesh, angels in burning bushes, prophets in fish stomachs, and—in my case—an encounter with Jesus at mile twenty of a marathon I won by losing.

Meeting Jesus at Mile Twenty

In 2011, I didn't like anything about the story the Lord was writing about me. In fact, it seemed he wasn't so much writing as attacking. His pen was a sword. He was stealing my hopes. Stomping on my dreams. The narrative of my life had taken a turn I never saw coming and certainly didn't want.

In February of that year, my wife said to me, "I don't love you anymore," and walked away. She had been the incarnation of my renewed hope, my second chance at life. After destroying my first marriage, my career, and my job a few years prior, I had been floundering in a sea of depression. Slowly drowning. She was the rope God had thrown to me. And I held on to it for dear life. I began smiling again. Dreamed again. Dared to hope once more. But when the divorce papers were signed, I began to sink even deeper than before. What's worse, I was embittered with the God who, in my eyes, had become the epitome of a heartless liar, a grand deceiver.

I decided that since God was evidently against me, I would be for myself. I needed something I could achieve by my own power and perseverance. A goal outside heaven's control. A trophy I could shove in the Lord's face that would show him, myself, and everyone else that I was not a washed-up failure.

For several years, running had been a passion. My chosen anti-depressant. I'd log the miles, feel the burn, sweat away the anger and stress. My speed had improved to the point where qualifying for the Boston Marathon was within my grasp. I poured my heart and soul into training over the course of the next year. Every morning, and sometimes twice a day, my feet would pound the pavement. I watched my diet, recorded my times, and incrementally worked my way toward the race in which I would qualify for the most famous marathon of all. And in so doing, recapture my story that the Lord had usurped and upended.

Adrenaline shot through my system as the starting pistol sounded early that November day. I was in corral number two, right behind the elite runners. Tens of thousands of others were lined up behind me. In the opening miles, my body fell into rhythm with the road. Today, I would prevail. The Lord may not delight in the strength of a horse, nor take pleasure in the legs of a man, but I certainly did (Ps. 147:10). I felt like one of those horses from the days of my youth, charging down the arena. My legs would carry me across the finish line in record time. Enough of this "the last shall be first" garbage. The first shall be first today. This race would prove, once and for all, that I had wrenched my story back from the hands of the Lord.

Right after I'd crossed the halfway point, when I was still on target to finish in under the three hour and fifteen minute goal, it happened. Like an open hand that gradually closes into a fist, my right hamstring slowly cramped into a ball of pain. I grabbed my leg, limped off the street, fell onto the sidewalk. My face contorted in pain. I stretched. Tried to walk. Stretched more. Gritted my teeth and pushed on. I would not fail. Not again. Not today.

I staggered past mile marker fifteen. Sixteen and seventeen were an agonizing blur. Every halting step put me further behind. Miles eighteen and nineteen sealed my fate. My dream race had devolved into a hobbling nightmare. Runner after runner passed me. My body had become a traitor. This day, reckoned to be my day of redemption, my chance to regain a little self-esteem, some self-worth, was crumbling before my eyes.

She came alongside me at mile twenty. A stranger. She jokingly asked if I could carry her the last six miles. Her foot was cramping. My leg was cramping. Pain forged an immediate bond between us. When I stopped to stretch for the hundredth time, she stopped and talked me forward. When she stopped and said she couldn't do this, I stopped and talked her forward. And forward we moved, gimping along, measuring progress no longer by miles but feet. Two weakened, faltering humans discovering that what we couldn't do alone, we could do solely on the strength of another.

As we climbed a hill and rounded a corner enveloped by cheering crowds, the last hundred yards of the race finally came into view. She reached over, took my hand, and held it high with hers as we crossed the finish line. And then, just like that, she vanished into the crowd. I searched for her to thank her, but she was gone. I don't even know her name. I can no longer hear her voice. I barely recall what she looked like. But this stranger, who carried me through the hardest six miles of my life—I know who she was.

Jesus met me at mile twenty that day. Met me in my failure. Met me in my pain, disappointment, weakness, anger, and self-loathing. He met me at the bottom in a stranger's voice who pushed me on. In a stranger's hand who took mine in her own. In a fellow sufferer who showed me that I was not alone. When I thought God was against me, I came face-to-face with the One who limps along with us in our pain.

I began that race to prove to the Lord that I didn't need him. That my life was my story. That he had no right to rewrite my narrative. And over the course of four and half hours, and 26.2 miles, the Lord showed me how wrong I was. What I needed was not a trophy but a cross. What I needed was not reliance upon my own strength but acceptance of my own weaknesses and trust in the strength of another. I didn't need to qualify for the Boston Marathon. I needed to realize that in losing myself, I would gain Christ. In ceasing to lean upon my own understanding, I would fall into the arms of a merciful God. My story was never my story. It was always, and remains, the story of Christ in me, with me, for me.

What does God want us to do with our lives? As we meander down the daily labyrinth of work and family and church, sometimes walking, sometimes stumbling, often falling flat on our faces, he wants us to realize that when we are weak, then he is strong. The less of us there is, the more there is of Christ in us. The more fragile our control is, the more we learn to trust in him.

The Lord commissions us all as his secret agents, as he did with Moses and Jonah and Paul, but these missions are not a chance to showcase our strength but rather the grace of the Lord who works within us. He is hidden in our simplicity, concealed in our crosses, to manifest himself as the God who doesn't work according to the ways of the world. He is writing our story in such a way that Christ is the central character—loving, forgiving, and working in us to show that whatever race we might be in, we'll cross the finish line by his strength alone. And in his victory, we triumph.

Discussion Questions

1. When you were growing up, how did you envision your future would be? Did it turn out that way? Discuss how our lives are more like a labyrinth than a blueprint. Do you agree or disagree with this quote, "Uncertainties are one of the most underappreciated gifts in life." Why or why not?

    _____

    _____

    _____

2. Review the first eight years of Moses' life, as it is recounted in Exodus 1-2, Hebrews 11:24-27, and Acts 7:20-28. Discuss how his first attempt to deliver his people backfired? He was forty years old then (Acts 7:23), but eighty years old when the Lord called him from the burning bush (Exodus 3). How was the older Moses the seemingly "wrong man" for the job? And why, because of that, was he God's choice?

    _____

    _____

    _____

3.   Read 1 Peter 2:9-10. What does it mean that Christians are part of the "royal priesthood"? How does that define and describe how God uses us in this world?

_____

_____

_____

4.   Read Philippians 3:20; Romans 12:2; John 18:36. How are the followers of Jesus those who hold "dual-citizenship," on earth and in heaven? Discuss the quote from John Kleinig, "[We are] extraordinary people, aliens working to promote God's gracious rule here on earth. Behind the front of our ordinary lives, we work as secret agents of the heavenly King." Describe some of the ways we are his "secret agents."

_____

_____

_____

5.   Review the story of Jonah. Why did this prophet initially refuse to go to Nineveh (Jonah 4:1-3)? God brought Jonah down, down, down, all the way to the depths of the sea. Why? What was he teaching him, and us? How does the Lord use "failures" and "fools" to bring about his will?

_____

_____

_____

6.   Read 2 Corinthians 1:8-10; 6:1-10; 12:7-10. What themes do these verses have in common? What do these verses say about how God uses our struggles and weaknesses?

_____

_____

_____

7. Summarize what it means for our lives to have dual narratives (God's and our own). What is the Lord's purpose in writing his story over our stories? Discuss the implications of this quote: "Christian maturity is not marked by independence but dependence." How is this the best news of all?

_____

_____

_____

8. In the section, "Meeting Jesus at Mile Twenty," Chad tells the story of how the Lord used a complete stranger to show him that what he needed was not reliance upon his own strength but acceptance of his own weaknesses and trust in the strength of another. Why is this such a difficult lesson for us to learn? How is the grace of Jesus at work in the midst of our failures and weaknesses?

_____

_____

_____

Five

Bringing a Knife to a Gunfight

From my front doorstep to the back entrance of the park was a little less than a mile. Every morning, for almost three years, I would gulp down a cup of coffee, lace up my shoes, and zigzag through the neighborhood streets until my feet hit dirt.

McAllister Park is 976 acres of moss-laden trees, meandering creeks, and herds of whitetail deer so tame you can pass within a few feet of them. An island of raw, rare beauty enveloped by a sea of asphalt in San Antonio.

I christened one of its many trails as my own. Baptized it with the sweat of a thousand runs. I would speed down its winding course, headphones blasting music, glancing down at my Garmin to ensure I was still on pace. Tunnel vision became second nature. A chosen blindness to everything but the run. One mile, two miles, ten. I might as well have been running on a treadmill in Gold's Gym, so fixated was I upon my speed and goals. The training program was all that mattered.

Until one day, suddenly exhausted, I slackened my pace. The headphones came off, the watch was ignored, and I forced myself to walk. Within a matter of minutes I realized this trail I thought I knew so well was really unfamiliar territory to me.

I looked up. A few feet away stood a great-grandfather of a tree, high and exalted, one of its enormous limbs home to a colony of honeybees that buzzed about its bark. I looked down. Near some dense undergrowth lay a rotting log where a family of pink and purple mushrooms sprouted. Farther along, I looked to the left, where I spotted a slight movement in the grass. There lay a fawn, almost invisible in her God-given camouflage, eyeing me with big brown innocent eyes. As I walked on, I saw a patch of flowers encircling a rusty bucket, and a fallen tree that perfectly bridged the gap from one bank of the creek to another.

Every few steps I would stop. Look. Listen. And discover something new.

All these gifts of simplicity and beauty God had woven into his natural world. Yet I had sped blindly past them, countless times, on my way to accomplishing a goal. An artificial goal, manufactured in my mind. When I slowed to a walk, opened my eyes, and looked *at* things instead of *through* them, the Creator showed me the work he had been doing while I was engrossed in doing my own.

I had used the trail for running, but truth be told, this wasn't really about staying healthy and fit. This was the training ground for my system of self-preservation. That's what running had become. I was endeavoring to outpace anxiety. To log enough miles to elude self-disappointment. To put distance between me and the pack of fears hounding me. If I kept to my program, maybe I could finally keep a little peace as well.

Running, in other words, had become a weapon in my arsenal to battle a legion of inner demons.

The day I slowed down and inspected God's fingerprints all around me, I glimpsed, for a moment, a truth I had ignored. I'm not talking about stopping to smell the proverbial roses. This was far different. A deeper truth was afoot.

I could run twenty miles a day down this trail, fine-tune my form, ramp up my speed. I could wear the best gear, listen to the most upbeat music, stick to my program with religious zeal. Yes, it would appear impressive. Anything in which I had invested so much effort was calculated to succeed, right? If there were a weapon that would work in the battle against my demons, then surely this was it.

Or I could admit a painful truth: all this training was a treadmill that got me no further down the road of healing. No matter how fast I ran, I was simply spinning in place. It was all artificial. A self-help project. A self-preservation program. Running was a weapon I was forging in the fires of my own energy. I needed something radically different. Something I didn't devise or plan or control.

I needed something simpler, more basic, a weapon more focused on the work God did than what I was doing.

When God beckoned me to peer past my plans onto the canvas of his creation, I began to see this truth: just as he planted the tree buzzing with bees, crafted the fawn in the grass, and gave life to the flowers around that rusting bucket, so he was at work in other ways that were beyond my control and manipulation.

When we are looking for a weapon to fight our battles, we gravitate toward the complicated, but God directs us to the simple. We tend to choose the man-made, but God guides us toward what he makes. We want a tool we can control and manipulate, but God says, *No, what you need is a tool of my creation, filled with my Spirit.*

The challenge is this: the weapons of the Lord, by which our battles are fought, don't look like they will work. They are underwhelming in appearance, like bringing a knife to a gunfight. They are plain, ordinary, everyday. Yet, as we have seen already, this is God's chosen way. Strength concealed beneath weakness. Glory beneath humility. Beauty beneath ugliness.

Swing open the door of the arsenal of heaven and what kinds of weapons will you see lined up? Shards of clay jars, torches, brass instruments, a piece of dead wood, a bowl of water, and—behind them all—a volume of words.

Such are the weapons Gideon discovered one day.

Gideon's Brass Band and Pottery Class

Of all the eccentric characters in the book of Judges, Gideon stands out because he himself didn't stand out. By his own estimation, he was an unremarkable man. Readily forgotten, easily overlooked. Certainly not the one we would have picked out of the crowd as the chosen savior of Israel.

When the angel of the Lord appeared to him and named him "mighty man of valor," Gideon probably glanced over his shoulder (Judg. 6:12). *Who, me?* "Please, Lord, how can I save Israel?" he protested. "Behold, my clan is the weakest in Manasseh, and I am the least in my father's house" (v. 15). A mighty man of valor? More like the runt of the litter, the uncoordinated kid always picked last for the team.

Fear and self-doubt hamstrung Gideon. Time and again he had to be reassured. When the angel insisted that God would be with him, that he would strengthen him, Gideon needed sign after sign to calm his nerves. When the Lord told him to demolish his father's idolatrous altar, he did it, but only under the cloak of darkness, "because he was too afraid of his family and the men of the town to do it by day" (v. 27). And right before a climactic battle, the Lord had to prop him up yet again. "If you are afraid to go down [against the enemy], go down to the camp with Purah your servant," he instructed (7:10). So Gideon snuck down to the camp and overheard an enemy retelling a dream he had about Gideon defeating them. That affirmation from an unexpected source finally steeled him for the attack.

Yet while bolstering his servant's confidence, God simultaneously seemed intent on undermining it. When the Israelites were preparing to battle the Midianites under Gideon's leadership, the Lord decided he had far too many soldiers. With such a large force, his people might think they'd pulled this off on their own. So the Lord whittled the number down, first from thirty-two thousand to ten thousand, then from ten thousand to a measly three hundred. And these weren't three hundred Spartans. No wonder Gideon was a nervous wreck.

This was bad enough, but God wasn't finished yet. He was about to drop the real bombshell.

These three hundred Israelites wouldn't march onto the field brandishing bows, swords, and spears but rather trumpets, torches, and clay jars. They'd look like a high school band lugging around their homework from pottery class. This had all the makings of a suicide mission.

God was sending a puny force, armed with ridiculous weapons, led by a sheepish general into a battle they couldn't win.

Yet they did. These three hundred men surrounded their adversaries in the small hours of the night. At Gideon's signal they smashed the jars, held high the torches, and blew the trumpets. Pandemonium erupted inside the Midianite camp. As they cried out and fled, "the LORD set every man's sword against his comrade and against all the army" (v. 22). In their bewildered state, the soldiers began massive self-extermination. The Israelites were the brass orchestra and lighting techs at the Midianite's self-induced funeral.

Gideon's story is a vivid reminder that God chooses weapons that, in our estimation, are weak and foolish. He handpicks simple armaments and unspectacular armor to equip us for battle. Why? He knows us better than we know ourselves. He knows how prone we are to "lean on [our] own understanding" (Prov. 3:5) so he rips away our understanding, letting us fall to the ground. Facedown in the dirt. He reminds us of our genesis and what we are made of. He reminds us that our forefather, Adam, is named after *adamah*, "dirt." How truly foolish it is to trust in ourselves, in dirt-people, whose wisdom, too, is dirt poor. More importantly, he lifts us from the ground and bids us lean on him. To learn true wisdom from him. And to receive, with faith, the simple weapons he places in our hands.

All the weapons the Lord provides us are forged in the same place: the fires of his Word. That, and that alone, is the source of their unexpected power. That divine Word breathed life into the clay jars, torches, and trumpets of Gideon's army. The Lord selected the common and made it uncommon by inscribing his signature upon it. These utensils became God's jars, God's torches, God's trumpets. While retaining the outward appearance of human simplicity, they were impregnated with the inner reality of divine authority by the Word.

Once that happens, these weapons are no longer under our control and subject to our manipulation but become gifts whereby the Spirit defends us from every foe, every inner demon, that stalks us in this life.

Our True Enemies

At a recent meeting in my congregation, on the agenda was not only how much to allocate for missions in the annual budget and which volunteers would organize the upcoming Trunk-or-Treat but also this: whether or not we would allow open carry of handguns in our Sunday morning services.

In a state law signed by Texas Governor Greg Abbot, beginning in January 2016, citizens who hold a Concealed Handgun License (CHL) can openly carry their firearms in most public places. Should a business or a religious establishment opt not to allow this, they are obliged to post large signs outside the building, informing those with a CHL that this is a gun-free zone.

The fact that a worshiper could walk up to the altar and kneel for the Eucharist with a Glock 19 strapped to his hip is a chilling reminder of the culture of fear in which we reside.

In response to the fear of violence saturating our society, what do we do? We arm ourselves, enroll in self-defense classes, carry pepper spray, install elaborate security systems in our homes. We practice emergency drills to ready ourselves for an active shooter on campus or in a workplace. We can't board an airplane without removing our shoes, subjecting all our belongings to a search, and standing with our arms in the air so a body imager can scan us from head to toe. We can't travel, go to school or church, or even eat popcorn and watch a movie without the unspoken fear that someone trigger-happy, delusional, or consumed with murderous hate is lurking nearby.

We don't want to be caught unaware, unarmed, or unprotected, so we take steps to ensure our safety. We weaponize. Lock doors. Install cameras. Erect barricades. On the one hand, these elaborate precautions are understandable and, to an extent, necessary for public and individual well-being.

Yet they give rise to an unexpected side-effect. We focus so much on external threats and our efforts to thwart them by means of our own devising that we grow blind to more sinister dangers and the simple, down-to-earth means our Lord provides to protect us from them.

Paul reminded the church in Ephesus—and us—of the greatest threat we face: "We do not wrestle against flesh and blood, but against the rulers, against the authorities, against the cosmic powers over this present darkness, against the spiritual forces of evil in the heavenly places" (Eph. 6:12). There is no watch list to ensure these spiritual forces of evil don't board a plane and fly to our city. They can't be recognized by dress or language or online activity. In fact, their chosen guise is often banal, even seemingly positive. The devil masquerades as an angel of light (2 Cor. 11:14). What's more, the demons can even use the weapons we devise as part of their arsenal against us.

As I ran on that trail, I was fleeing from the spiritual forces of evil. From the demons of despair, shame, and guilt. But my program of self-protection—really of self-salvation—was not working. In fact, this weapon was working against me because I assumed that helping myself was the path toward healing. I thought I needed to tap into a reservoir of inner strength. To believe in myself.

That's precisely what the cosmic forces over this present darkness want us to do. The more we turn inward, the deeper into enemy territory we wander. The more I relied on my training program, my grit and sweat, my endeavors to redeem my wasted life, the more I transformed my heart into a darkened temple for the angel of light.

When we feel adrift in a sea of hopelessness, our tendency is to attempt to create an identity for ourselves that will prevent us from drowning in despair. We pour ourselves into work, clocking fifty, sixty, seventy hours at a job that will pronounce us important and indispensable. We starve ourselves to lose weight or pound our bodies at the gym so that we feel desirable, so that someone will notice us and love us. We attach ourselves to people—even marry them—who will infuse our empty lives with meaning. If all else fails, we get high on the narcotic of nostalgia, daydreaming of former glory or happy days when we meant something.

I've crafted all these weapons at one time or another, as most of us have. What we're really doing is arming ourselves against the spiritual forces of despair and self-loathing. But we're flirting with disaster. As long as our focus remains upon these artificial means of protecting the citadel of our ego, we're only playing into the hands of dark cosmic forces that drive us further and further away from the very One who holds the armor and weapons to protect us.

The Liquid Armor of God

After Paul pinpoints the greatest threats that face us, he tells us how to arm ourselves against them. We fasten on the belt of truth and breastplate of righteousness. Slip on the shoes of the gospel of peace. Take up the shield of faith and put on the helmet of salvation. We carry the sword of the Spirit, which is the Word of God. And we pray at all times in the Spirit (Eph. 6:14–18).

Most importantly, however, is Paul's opening remark. He says, "Take up the whole armor *of God*" (v. 13, emphasis added). Not "take up your whole armor." Not "take up the armor you have created or purchased." But put on God's armor. Hold his weapons. Be covered head to toe in the protection he provides.

Heaven's armor is not a system of efforts we put forth to fight battles with our demons of fear, regret, shame, and addiction. It's not the armor of self-help, self-worth, or self-motivation. There's nothing artificial or complicated about it.

In fact, every article of protection and defense can be reduced to one simple element: water.

When Jesus went into the desert to battle Satan, the water of the Jordan was still dripping from his head. After he was baptized, "the Spirit immediately drove him into the wilderness. And he was in the wilderness forty days, being tempted by Satan" (Mark 1:12–13). He marched into enemy territory clothed with liquid armor. After he was baptized, the Spirit alighted upon him "like a dove," and the Father pronounced, "You are my beloved Son" (vv. 10–11).

Drenched in the Father's favor, filled with his Spirit, Jesus was armed for conflict with the demons. In fact, as church father Cyril of Jerusalem describes it, the conflict had already begun in the Jordan. He depicts the baptism of Jesus as his descent into the waters, where he "chained fast the strong one, so that we might gain the power to tread on scorpions and serpents," in other words, our own enemies.[1] War was happening already in the water. And victory was secured.

The Father's chosen means to ready us for every battle we face is as ordinary as the stuff we use to wash dirty dishes. We are "baptized into Christ Jesus"; that is, "we were buried therefore with him by baptism into death, in order that, just as Christ was raised from the dead by the glory of the Father, we too might walk in newness of life" (Rom. 6:3–4).[2] Our "old self was crucified with him" (v. 6) when liquid nails affixed us to his cross. And our new self, re-created in the image of Christ, was resurrected in those same waters.

We put on the armor of God when the Father puts Christ on us in baptism. The truth of our adoption by him wraps around us as a belt. The righteousness of Jesus is our breastplate. The water poured over our heads is a helmet. The shoes of the gospel of peace are the good news that we walk in his favor. The shield of faith extinguishes all the flaming darts of the evil one because it is wet with the water of Christ's fidelity to us. And the sword of the Spirit, the Word of God, is that Word that says the same thing to us as it said to Jesus in the Jordan: "You are my beloved son. You are my beloved daughter." Because "in Christ Jesus you are all sons of God, through faith. For as many of you as were baptized into Christ have put on Christ" (Gal. 3:26–27).

Armed with Christ, covered by his grace, we are safe. We are safe in a way no self-devised program can make us. The identities we crave, the worth we desire, are answered when the Father pronounces us his children in baptism. The love we long for fills us when the Spirit washes us into the grace of Jesus. Instead of seeking approval and attraction by subjecting our bodies to workout routines and rigorous training schedules, we can hear our Father say, "I love you as you are. Overweight or thin. The girl next door or the beauty queen. Wrinkled or Botoxed. You are now part of the body of my Son. I see you only in him. And because you are in him, I see you as spotless, resplendent, holy."

While our tendency is to focus inward—to what we can do, to the artificial means of protection we devise—God is always bending our eyes outward to Jesus, who arms us in baptism by wrapping himself around us.

It's all so profoundly simple—so simple we find it hard to swallow. Like the clay jars, trumpets, and torches of Gideon, there's nothing glorious about water. We shower in it, flush our toilets with it, use it to keep our grass green. Yet that's why our Father chooses it. Because it's ordinary. Because it's unimpressive. Because it's the perfect mask behind which he can hide to do extraordinary things to us and for us. It's like Gideon's utensils, like a Roman cross, and like the staff of Moses.

The Staff of God

When we talked earlier about Moses, there's one element of his story we only alluded to. Not only did the Lord use this ordinary man with an ordinary job to rescue the Israelites from slavery but he armed him with an ordinary piece of wood. Wielding only a shepherd's crook, Moses fought against the most powerful leader of the most powerful nation on earth. God sent him in with a stick to chop down a forest.

"What is that in your hand?" God asked Moses (Exod. 4:2).

"A staff," he replied.

"Throw it on the ground," he said (v. 3).

And when Moses did, it became a serpent. Later, Moses and Aaron would use this staff to swallow the staffs of Pharaoh's magicians (7:8–13), to turn the Nile into blood (v. 19), to infest the land with frogs (8:5), and to transform Egyptian dust into swarming gnats (8:16). In the climactic encounter between the Israelites and the Egyptians, Moses held his staff over the waters of the Red Sea to open them up so his people could pass through, then to zip them up once more, like a massive body bag, over the pursuing Egyptians. Armed with a dead piece of wood, Moses pulled off the greatest military victory in biblical history.

How he did this is disclosed in a single verse: When Moses journeyed into Egypt, he "took the staff of God in his hand" (4:20). As he did with Gideon's jars, trumpets, and torches, the Lord claimed this stick as his own. It became the staff of God. He sanctified it, made it holy, filled the simple with the profound. The rod embodied the mighty hand and the outstretched arm of Yahweh, of which Deuteronomy frequently speaks (e.g., Deut. 7:19).[3]

A Jewish tradition says this rod was one of ten objects formed at twilight on the eve of the first Sabbath of creation. But it was nothing so profound. It was a plain tree limb, chopped down, dried, and fashioned into a shepherd's tool and weapon. There was nothing impressive about it, certainly nothing magical. Its power came from God's claim upon it. It was a vehicle for his gracious work in this world. The staff "spoke" God's saving, protecting will into existence for his people.

When we're engaged in some type of struggle—spiritual, emotional, or relational—we all tend to assume that the bigger and splashier some means of rescue is, the better it will work. Sign up for an online seminar about spiritual warfare. Devour bestselling books about how to totally revamp our lives to overcome barriers and achieve remarkable success. Train our minds to think positive, to name and claim victory. Some of us end up in churches where worship is a series of shock and awe services where the power of the Spirit is supposedly on display.

All of this is designed to impress. And it usually does—temporarily, at least. But God's chosen means of rescue, his weapons, are never going to impress you. They will, however, save you.

The weapons of God always direct you away from yourself. The Lord's purpose in diminishing the forces of Gideon and arming him with such foolish instruments was to ensure that the Israelites were emptied of any false hope that they could achieve victory on the basis of their prowess in battle. The weapons were a visible reminder that they couldn't look to themselves. God would be fighting for them under the guise of weak instruments. Likewise, when Israel panicked at the Red Sea as they saw the Egyptian army approaching, Moses, standing there with the staff in his hand, said, "Fear not, stand firm, and see the salvation of the LORD, which he will work for you today. . . . The LORD will fight for you, and you have only to be silent" (Exod. 14:13–14). In other words, hurry up and do nothing. Through his staff he will work salvation for you.

Doing nothing is the hardest thing for us to do. We'd rather talk nonstop for hours than be utterly silent for a few minutes. We'd rather be told to plan this, accomplish that, busy ourselves with these goals, than simply to receive the work the Lord does for us. It all seems too easy. Too childish. Too much like we have no part to play in our own defense, recovery, and ultimate salvation.

But we don't. And that's the best of news! We are the recipients of the Lord's labor. The Lord will save you and you have only to be trapped. The Lord will forgive you and you have only to be a sinner. The Lord will give you a new identity, cleanse you of every spot of shame, and fill you with an inner peace that this world cannot give. And you have only to do nothing. The new person we are in Christ, says author and pastor R. J. Grunewald, "has empty hands, clinging to nothing but the work of Jesus."[4] Our empty, outstretched hands of faith are filled with the gracious work of Jesus.

The staff of Moses, the jars of Gideon, the waters of baptism—they are all the unpretentious ways our Lord chooses to defend us. Each of them, in their own way, are the Word of God made visible. A word of wood. A word of pottery. A liquid word. They are not the words we would look for, or even hope for, but they are the words of life itself. And they are the words that are formed on the cross of Christ himself.

"Jews demand signs and Greeks seek wisdom," Paul says, but "we preach Christ crucified" (1 Cor. 1:22–23). We demand performance, entertainment, quick fixes, and processed spirituality packed with the fat and sugar of this world's wisdom. We want a checklist of things we can do to defend ourselves, improve ourselves, to feel safe in this world because we are in control. But God draws us to Christ crucified. To a bloodstained, dead piece of wood upon which hangs the Lord of life. To a broken vessel from which streams the light of victory. To a cry, "It is finished," that blasts like a trumpet through the night of this fallen world to announce that our sin is forgiven, our death has died, and every demon has been defanged and debarked by the crushing blow of the saving sacrifice of God himself.

We stream into the crucified Christ on the river of baptism. When he died, water and blood flowed from his side. When we are crucified and buried with him in baptism, his watery blood clothes us with his own righteousness. When you see a baptism take place, it seems child's play. A little water splashed, a few words spoken. But in that bath is hidden the armor of the Almighty. The helmet of salvation, the breastplate of righteousness, the belt of truth, the gospel shoes, the shield of faith. And in our mouths is placed the sword of the Spirit, the Word of God, by which every evil assault is vanquished.

Three plain words—*I am baptized*—send all of hell into a tailspin. That trinity of words defeats the demons within us because they name us as the Father's child.

I speak them when I get up in the morning to remind myself that though I struggle against temptation, I have a Lord who was crucified for me. I speak them as I drive to work to remind myself that no matter what obstacle the day may hold, I am safe in the love of my Savior. I tell myself, *I am baptized*, when the demons of my past try to turn my present into a war of self-hatred and self-pity, because I know that my past immoralities and lies have been washed into the sea of Christ's grace. And I say them at night, as I reflect back upon my failures of the day, because I know that the Father sees me in Jesus as perfect and whole.

58

In her book *Liturgy of the Ordinary*, Tish Harrison Warren writes,

> As Christians, we wake each morning as those who are baptized. We are united with Christ and the approval of the Father is spoken over us. We are marked from our first waking moment by an identity that is given to us by grace: an identity that is deeper and more real than any other identity we will don that day.[5]

This identity defines who we are and whose we are. It covers us from the moment the alarm clock sounds until our head hits the pillow at night. It even guards us as we sleep. Awake or dreaming, these three words shield us: *I am baptized.*

Our lives are complicated. They are often a disaster. We wrestle against the spiritual forces of evil in the heavenly places that seek to slither inside our fractured hearts. But our Lord's defense of us is uncomplicated. He simply says, *You are mine. I have baptized you into my Son. No demon, no guilt, no despair can change or diminish my love for you.*

What I realized, years ago, on that running trail is what I realize anew every single day. We don't need a spiritual weapon we devise or control. We don't need an arsenal full of stunning spiritual artillery that we can manipulate to rescue ourselves. We need what we already have: God's work done on our behalf. A tool of his creation, pregnant with his Spirit.

We have the cross of baptism shaping us into the sons and daughters of the Father. We have the true words of the Spirit shielding us from every accusation of the father of lies. We have Jesus—or, rather, Jesus has us. And he fights for us with a zeal fired by unquenchable love. Rest in the sacred simplicity of an identity that is yours in him. Rest in the peace of knowing that nothing depends on you but all on him. Rest in the water of baptism, in the Word of his favor, which unites you to a cross in which you are armed with the grace of heaven.

Discussion Questions

1. Reflect on this quote: "When we are looking for a weapon to fight our battles, we gravitate toward the complicated, but God directs us to the simple." What are some of our favorite self-help projects or self-preservation programs that we like to use to "fix ourselves"? Why do we often prefer these to God's ways?

_____

_____

_____

2. Read or review the story of Gideon, especially in Judges 6-7. How would you characterize him and his personality? What were his weaknesses? How did the Lord respond to those weaknesses? Why would God choose someone to lead the army who obviously struggled with fear? Discuss what we can learn from this today.

    _____

    _____

    _____

3. Why did the Lord make Gideon reduce the size of his army (Judges 7:2)? With what strange "weapons" did Gideon arm his warriors (7:16)? Talk about why the Lord arranged the battle as he did. What was the true power behind the weapons that were used? What implications does that have for the life of the church today?

    _____

    _____

    _____

4. Read Ephesians 6:10-12 and 2 Corinthians 11:14. Discuss how our focus on external, physical threats and our efforts to thwart them can blind us to more sinister, spiritual dangers and the means God has provided to protect us. Why do our spiritual enemies want us to turn inward, to rely on ourselves?

    _____

    _____

    _____

5. Read Ephesians 6:13-17. Discuss each of these elements of armor and what they imply. Why is it important to note this armor is "of God"?

    _____

    _____

    _____

6. Read Romans 6:3-11 and Galatians 3:26-27. Using the language of these texts, describe what God does for us in baptism. How does baptism clothe us with the armor of Jesus? How does our Father use baptism to direct us not inward, to ourselves, but outward, to Jesus?

    _____

    _____

    _____

7. Read Exodus 4:1-5; 4:17-20; 7:8-13, 19; 8:5, 16; 14:13-16. According to these verses, what all did God do through the staff of Moses? What was the Lord teaching the Israelites, and us, by using such a simple, unpretentious piece of wood to work such miracles? How does that staff lead us to the cross?

    _____

    _____

    _____

8. Discuss how the three words, "I am baptized," can send all of hell into a tail-spin. How does baptism establish our identity in Christ? How does the Lord use baptism to shape us into his sons and daughters?

    _____

    _____

    _____

Six

Saints John and Jane Doe

As we drive to the service, the grass alongside the roadway has quieted to a subdued brown but the trees chatter in multicolored speech. A few weeks from now the aroma of roasting turkey will waft from the kitchen. And just last night, costumed children filed up to our door to ask for a treat.

It's that time of year. Nature goes into hibernation, families plan holidays, and the church gathers to remember the forgotten.

The first day of November is one of the most uplifting, yet underappreciated, days in the church year. For traditions like mine that pattern their worship around a liturgical calendar, this day is called All Saints' Day.

It's a different kind of holy day. Scattered throughout the year, on certain days, we remember the lives and deaths of well-known believers. Saint Patrick, missionary to Ireland, on March 17. Saint Monica, mother of Augustine, on August 27. Saint Andrew, apostle of Jesus, on November 30. We may not know everything about these people, but we know enough. We know their names and approximately when they lived. We recount stories and traditions about them. We even sing songs about them. In the culture of the church at least, these saints are famous.

But November 1 is not for the famous. It's for the unfamous, the forgotten, the unknown and overlooked. The little people boxed up in the attic of the church's memory. People for whom the mystic chords of memory will not swell into a chorus throughout the centuries. No one will compose hymns about them or craft prayers in their memory. They are Saints Sue and Barbara. Saints Gary and Frank. Saints John and Jane Doe.

All Saints' Day is the day the church remembers to remember the forgotten.

The day the church remembers to remember people like most of us.

A couple of years ago my family vacationed near Gatlinburg, Tennessee. As we snaked our way down one of the narrow roads in the Smoky Mountains, we spotted a tiny cemetery, half secluded in dense foliage. We parked the car and walked among the weathered gravestones. One bore the dates March 12, 1898–March 14, 1898. The inscription was as simple as it was sorrowful: "Infant Son of Thomas and Margaret Fitzpatrick." He was given no name. A cross with the words "Asleep in Jesus" was etched underneath. On All Saints' Day, we remember to remember this boy.

On New Year's Eve of this past year, my wife and I spent the day in downtown San Antonio. We rode in a boat that gave us a floating tour of the River Walk. We enjoyed some seafood, sipped a margarita later in the evening, and watched as the night sky blazed with dazzling fireworks as the clock struck midnight. Early the next morning, sleepy-eyed, we strolled through the streets near the Alamo. The hubbub of the night before was now muted. City workers, clad in orange vests, scurried about everywhere. Emptying trash bins, picking up beer cans, sweeping up cigarette butts. None of us were thinking about them the night before. Such children of God labor forgotten, virtually anonymous. On All Saints' Day, we also remember to remember people like these—those who, in their earthly lives, were busy cleaning up the messes of the world.

We remember to remember the unknown farmers and ranchers who worked to put food on our table. The craftsman who built the table to hold the plates of food. The builders who constructed the house in which the table sits. The surveyors who mapped the square feet of the lot where the house was built. And the men and women who footed the bill for it all. People we will never know whose vocations, investments, and know-how made a simple meal in our simple home possible. Servants of the Lord who did their job, got paid, and went home to families of their own. We remember to remember them all.

All Saints' Day flattens the hierarchy of holiness we often assume exists in the kingdom of God. We don't just remember the bigwig saints but every believer who is part of the assembly John beheld: "a great multitude that no one could number, from every nation, from all tribes and peoples and languages, standing before the throne and before the Lamb, clothed in white robes, with palm branches in their hands" (Rev. 7:9). November 1 democratizes this vast throng of believers, saying of that son of Thomas and Margaret Fitzpatrick, of those who cleaned up other people's messes, and of every child of God who fell through the cracks of the world, "You matter. You are important. You are not just a statistic, a body, a number. Jesus was thinking of you as he hung upon the cross. Our Father knows you by name."

All Saints' Day, however, is not just an annual remembrance of those who have departed this veil of tears but a vivid reminder for all of us who are still slogging our way through it. We remember to remember that we are never forgotten by God. Not for a millisecond do we slip his mind. Even the most diligent of moms and dads have moments when their children are not in the forefront of their minds. "Can a woman forget her nursing child?" God asks Zion. Then he responds, "Even these may forget, yet I will not forget you. Behold, I have engraved you on the palms of my hands" (Isa. 49:15–16). God isn't simply aware that we exist. He sat in the chair of a tattoo artist to have our names inked into his skin.

As I drive to church to attend the All Saints' Day service, I know and believe all this. And at the same time I doubt and disbelieve it.

As good as it sounds, it also sounds too good to be true. Around seven billion people populate our world. Who am I to think that even an all-powerful God notices me among so many? The only chance I have of being known is to do something that catches the eye of my Lord.

As I stare out the window at the brown grass and multicolored trees, I see in both these icons of autumn what so often determines the decisions I make. The dying grass is emblematic not only of the brevity of my life but how dull and colorless it usually is. I get up, go to work, come home, crawl into bed, then repeat it all the next day. A nagging sense of unaccomplishment bedevils me. A brown grass kind of existence over which hangs a lackluster cloud of anonymity.

So out of a looming sense that I must do something that sets me apart, that makes me special, I strive to add some flash, some vibrancy, to my life. What I need are more chromatic trees in the drab lawn of my bio. A dab of fame. A trophy case I can display. Anything that will catch the eye of others—and God—and make them say, "Now there's a guy who's made a name for himself."

Anonymity easily degenerates into a phobia, doesn't it? We sometimes battle this fear by engineering our own little towers of Babel. The ancient workers who settled in the land of Shinar constructed the world's first skyscraper, saying, "Let us make a name for ourselves" (Gen. 11:4). God named Adam. This man named the animals and later his wife. Eve named Cain and Seth. No one picked their own name out of a baby book. It was given by another. But the tower builders wanted to reverse this. They would make a name for themselves. They would concoct something great, something that stood out. The tower was the incarnation of their ego. It said, "Look at us. We are important. See what we have accomplished."

But towers of Babel, in the old world as in the new, give rise only to confusion. The Lord shuffled the language deck of these builders. They made a name for themselves all right, just not the one they envisioned. Rather than being a hallmark of their achievement, the unfinished tower was branded Babel—a babbling, blubbering logo of the foolish human quest for fame. God knew better than to let them have their way. "Nothing that they propose to do will now be impossible for them," he said (v. 6). In other words, tower-building and name-creating held within them the possibilities of even more magnificent disasters.

The phobia of anonymity is the breeding ground of projects that we think will do us good, but God knows will only engender harm. He's not a bully on the beach who kicks over our sand castles. He's a Father who sees below the surface to what really fuels our efforts. We want to be known. To be noticed. To be more than one of those countless faces that blur past on the fast-moving subway of human existence. So even while he frustrates our tower-building plans, he reaches out in love to address the root of the problem.

He reminds us, again and again, that all efforts to make a name for ourselves are not only in vain but are totally unnecessary. He is at work transforming our minds so that, first of all, we see our anonymity not as a phobia but a mirage. He not only knows us and calls us by name, he outdoes himself by keeping a running tally on how many hairs are on our heads (Matt. 10:30). He knows the narratives embedded within our every scar. Even before the moment of our conception, in his book the days of our life story were "written, every one of them, the days that were formed for [us], when as yet there was none of them" (Ps. 139:16). We are far from being unknown by the Creator. He knows our story better than we know it ourselves. We are all household names in heaven.

But that's only part of how our Father is transforming our minds. More importantly, he is teaching us to see our place and importance in this world with fresh eyes. He turns our gaze away from the complicated blueprints for our self-exalting towers to the blank page of common, everyday existence. What will we write and draw on this day's page? Rather than mind-blowing achievements that will turn people's heads, he bids us fill that page with little sacrificial acts for others that are imbued with the humble glory of the cross. Labor at your job. Kiss your spouse. Call your mom. Invite a coworker to church. Take out the trash. Buy a burger for a homeless person. Help your kids with homework. Donate some clothes to a thrift store. Visit a sick friend in the hospital.

Rather than writing in calligraphy on the blank page of this day's life, print simple words in block letters that spell out a life of self-emptying love.

Drummed into our heads all day every day by our culture is the liturgy of self-achievement. In *Life of the Beloved*, Henri J. M. Nouwen writes of the loud voices that demand, "Prove that you are worth something; do something relevant, spectacular, or powerful, and then you will earn the love you so desire."[1] You know the mantras. Second place is last place. Push yourself to outperform others. Stand out from the crowd. Make your life worthy of an inspirational meme. Be ambitious. Be somebody.

But there is another voice that speaks a far different word. "Make it your ambition to lead a quiet life" (1 Thess. 4:11 NIV). "When you give to the needy, do not let your left hand know what your right hand is doing, so that your giving may be in secret. And your Father who sees in secret will reward you" (Matt. 6:3–4). "Do nothing from selfish ambition or conceit, but in humility count others more significant than yourselves" (Phil. 2:3). "Do not be haughty, but associate with the lowly. Never be wise in your own sight" (Rom. 12:16). "If anyone would be first, he must be last of all and servant of all" (Mark 9:35).

In the church, anonymity is the greatest fame of all.

In times past, as now, Jesus rolls up his sleeves and goes to work in this world as one with "no form or majesty that we should look at him, and no beauty that we should desire him" (Isa. 53:2). He is the "God who hides himself" (45:15). He razes glorious towers but embraces a shameful cross. He "has brought down the mighty from their thrones and exalted those of humble estate" (Luke 1:52).

Those of humble estate. Those like an unnamed girl from Israel whose simple service changed one man's life forever. A girl whom God employs to remind us of the mysterious ways he works in our own lives.

The Unnamed Heroine in Syria

She was young, the kind of girl who climbs aboard a yellow school bus every morning with her pink backpack and turns to smile and wave at us.

But she didn't wave at her family the day that changed her life forever. No school bus drove her to classrooms and a playground. She was a victim of kidnapping, ripped away from her mom and dad, brothers and sisters, toys and bed and every other detail that defined her life. The northern neighbors of Israel, the Syrians, "on one of their raids had carried off [this] little girl" (2 Kings 5:2). And she wouldn't be going home. Not soon. Not ever.

That's the way it worked. A new life, a new language, a new culture, an old problem: violence and greed once more turned the life of an innocent victim inside out. Back home, she would have grown up, probably married a local man from her tribe, and raised little boys and girls of her own. But now she was property, human chattel, subject to the whims of her captors. She had every reason to believe that her life was now pointless and hopeless. Whatever she may have once dreamed of doing and being had been crushed underfoot. It's highly likely that even the most personal identifier of who she was—her Hebrew name—was changed.

But we don't know her name. She is Jane Doe. An anonymous little servant girl.

I suspect none of us have experienced any trauma as life-changing as she did. And yet many of us have undergone traumatic experiences of our own that forever redefine our lives. The fracture of family cohesion in the explosion of a messy divorce. Foster children shifted from home to home. The unplanned pregnancy in our teenage years that sent our lives into a tailspin. Years trapped in an abusive relationship that left an indelible stamp upon our psyche. We wonder, as perhaps she did, how any good can come of our lives. Any chance we had is now destroyed. We look in the mirror and see what we assume everyone else sees: a nobody, a lost cause, a body that simply takes up space on a planet already overcrowded with expendable people.

Of all the places our little friend could have ended up, she became the property of a prestigious military family. Her master, Naaman, boasted an impressive list of achievements. He was "commander of the army of the king of Syria," the ancient equivalent of our Chairman of the Joint Chiefs of Staff. He was "a great man with his master and in high favor, because by him the LORD had given victory to Syria," and "he was a mighty man of valor" (v. 1).

He had it all: prestige, honor, success, power, influence. He was a force to be reckoned with. Unlike his servant girl, Naaman is named and known. The kind of guy his hometown throws a parade for. The kind of person who stands in front of the mirror, smiles, and says, "Now there's someone who's made a name for himself."

And yet when Naaman looked in that mirror, he saw something else. Something he didn't want to see. He stared at splotches on his skin, scabs and scales that no Syrian doctor could cure. For all his seeming greatness, this man "was a leper" (v. 1).

It's hard to feel sorry for Naaman. If we feel anything, it's that German expression, *Schadenfreude*, pleasure we derive from someone else's misfortune. A kind of vicious joy. *Serves you right*, we think. *You kidnapped this girl but you're a prisoner of your own disease.* I'll be honest: were I in her shoes, every time I spotted the general scratching at his wilting skin my heart would probably have twisted into a smirk.

But I am not her, and—thank God—she was not like me. The Lord gave to this servant girl a perspective I desperately need. A perspective we all need.

She "worked in the service of Naaman's wife," we're told (v. 2). The woman who shared a bed with Naaman, who perceived the depths of suffering in her husband as only a wife can. Perhaps one day the mistress of the house was openly lamenting about her husband's plight. "Another doctor, another failed remedy. It's getting worse. We'd move heaven and earth to find a cure. But everywhere we go, it's just another dead end." And the girl who had lost everything, whom we might assume silently gloated over her master's disease, shows us what true love sounds like. "Would that my lord were with the prophet who is in Samaria!" she announced. "He would cure him of his leprosy" (v. 3).

Of all this girl had spoken, or would speak for the remainder of her life, this exclamation alone is recorded. Her speech, in Hebrew, is a mere ten words. Yet compressed within them are ten thousand nouns of faith and verbs of hope. A whole language of redemption, of freedom from pain and shame. She didn't have to say them. But they burst forth voluntarily from her lips. The Hebrew for "would that" could be rendered, "Oh! If only!" "Oh! If only Naaman would make a trip back to my homeland. If only he would pay a visit to this prophet I know. If only he did that, the God of this prophet, my God, Yahweh, would heal him. Oh! If only!"

The most remarkable part of this story is not the pilgrimage Naaman would later make to the prophet in Israel. Nor even his subsequent healing in the waters of the Jordan. No, the most remarkable part is that this powerful general, this mighty man of valor before whom armies had fallen, discovers in the words of an anonymous little slave girl the hope he found nowhere else. Naaman's wife relayed to him what she said. He then went and found his own lord, the king of Syria. And he said to him, "Thus and so spoke the girl from the land of Israel" (v. 4). And the king responded, "Go now, and I will send a letter to the king of Israel" (v. 5).

Picture that. Two men with international power and prestige, a general and a king, engaging in conversation about the words of a powerless girl. And not only conversing but believing. And not only believing but heaping all their hopes upon the narrow shoulders of her confession.

Her speech forever altered the course of Naaman's life. He embarked on the journey. After being somewhat mulish at first, he eventually submitted to the prophet's strange command. "He went down and dipped himself seven times in the Jordan." As a result "his flesh was restored like the flesh of a little child, and he was clean" (v. 14). Did you catch that? His flesh became like the flesh of a "little child." Like the flesh of the "little girl" who sent him there. The Hebrew phrases are virtually identical: she was a *na'arah qetanah* and he became like a *na'ar qaton*.

A divine reversal took place. The proud master was humbled, lowered, made little, so that he became the spitting image of the humble, low little girl who served him. The first became the last, the greatest the least. In a land not his own, in a river he thought inferior, heeding a command he considered foolish, Naaman finally arrived at the place where God wanted him to be all along.

The heroine of this story is Saint Jane Doe. Yet she wouldn't have considered herself a heroine. Just a servant. Just the lips of the Lord he used to speak the right words at the right time to a fellow human in need. We don't know her name but we know the name of the God who knew her. The Lord who remembered to remember her when it seemed she was forgotten by everyone else in the world. And the Lord who, in his mercy, remembers to remember us, and to use our lives and callings in small ways to accomplish things great and small in his world.

Football, Stats, and Sacraments

There's a peaceful rivalry in our home between my sixteen-year-old son, Luke, who is a fan of the Green Bay Packers, and my wife and me, who cheer for the Dallas Cowboys. When neither team is playing, we usually root for the underdog. Like all armchair quarterbacks, we critique passes and blocks and kicks as if we could have done better had we been on the field. And we half listen to the professional announcers, many of whom are former football players themselves, rattle off statistic after statistic, many of which are so esoteric you feel like you've entered the football twilight zone. Something like, "Tom Johnson was the first NFL draft pick in the past five seasons to run forty yards to a touchdown on an interception with ten seconds left in the third quarter during overtime in a preseason game opener." Wait, what?

Upon hearing one such stat this weekend, my son turned to me and said, "You know, Dad, it's like they have to make up statistics for everything, to determine whether a player is special or significant." Luke was more right than he probably realized. And not just about football.

We live, work, and even socialize in a culture that keeps statistics about us—measures us, quantifies us, weighs us, collects data about us—to determine whether we're worthy of being accorded any significance or inclusion. The sacraments of American religion are all numerical in nature. We are judged worthy or unworthy based upon performance, output, and productivity. Stats are our salvation or damnation. They determine whether we're worthy, or unworthy, of being on a given team.

In a best-case scenario, our stats justify us. But then we're pressed to ramp it up even more. Make more money. Score more clients. Lose more weight. Buy a home in a more affluent neighborhood. In a worst-case scenario, our stats condemn us. Maybe we're given a chance to redeem ourselves. Or maybe we're thrown under the bus and replaced by someone with more potential. So even when we win, we lose, because we never reach that tantalizing quota that will unalterably secure our position. And, along with it, our sense of worth, peace, and belonging.

In the kingdom of the almighty number, where the first are first and even the second are last, we remember only the names of those who are the cream of the crop.

In the kingdom of the humble Christ, where the first are last and the last are first, God remembers even the names of those who sink to the bottom.

For in the church, we win by losing, are humbled to be exalted, receive a name even when lost in anonymity.

This is a hard truth for us to learn because it runs counter to every pseudo-truth we hear from society, our coworkers, sometimes our own church or family. But loudest of all is the voice coming from within. The Lord is our Shepherd, but we still want. And one of the things we want is to separate from the fold and blaze trails of fame for our name's sake. Though our help is in the name of the Lord, we suppose it would help if our own name were well-known, applauded, coveted. John the Baptist's words about Jesus, "He must increase, but I must decrease" (John 3:30), declare war against our ingrained proclivity to self-exaltation.

So God does with us what he's always done with his beloved people: he crucifies us. He hammers our ego to the wood of suffering. He puts a crown of thorns on our big heads. He strips us of our clothing of self-importance. And there, naked, dying, bleeding, we realize that we are not on the cross alone. God himself is there, naked, dying, and bleeding alongside us. Or, rather, we in him and he in us. He is bringing us down with him—down to the depths of death itself. He is undoing us that he might redo us. Dead and buried, unnamed and unknown, in the pits of oblivion with God incarnate, we discover, as did Naaman, that we have arrived at the place God wanted us to be all along.

That general became like the little girl who sent him into those waters. We become like the Christ who crucifies us with himself. Our identities are subsumed into his own. And as we walk forth from the Jordan of the tomb, we step onto the dry ground of Easter as new creations, with our flesh and soul and mind and spirit the spitting image of Jesus himself.

On God's field, the only statistic that determines how special or significant we are is the one that computes the work of Jesus. His victories are our victories. His trophies are our trophies. He shares his glory with us, not as members of his team but as members of his own body. All that is his is ours, including his name.

My name is Chad. You have yours. But all those baptized in the name of the Father and of the Son and of the Holy Spirit have been christened with a better name: Christian.

Christian: one who is of Christ, one who is in Christ, one who shares the very name of the Son of the Father, anointed by the Spirit, an heir of heaven. Christian: one whose worth and importance are not in himself or herself but in the one whose name we bear.

And in bearing that name, we are assured that we are never anonymous in the eyes of our Father. Be we President of the United States or a pipeline welder, a gold-medal swimmer or a stay-at-home mom who watches her kids run through the sprinkler on a hot summer day. Every minuscule detail in our lives, in our vocations, has God dancing for joy over the works of his hands. He is like the dad who cheers when his toddler first learns how to spoon mashed potatoes into her mouth. Nothing is too small for him to notice, nothing too unimportant for him to photograph and frame in the hallways of his memory. We are his children, his Christians, the workers in his vineyard, where he is pleased with one grape or a thousand in our buckets. All our works, big and little, known and unknown, coalesce into perfection when they are folded into the labor of Jesus.

Every day millions of us labor unnoticed on the few acres of soil where God has planted us to do his work. I drive a truck and do a little writing. Perhaps you teach or clean teeth or pastor a flock. No one will ever throw a parade in our honor. We serve, like little Jane Doe, out of the limelight, sometimes in the shadows of great persons like Naaman. But with us is a light unseen. A light that has shone in our hearts to give us the light of the knowledge of the glory of God in the face of Christ. The glow of that light illumines our lives in a way imperceptible to the world. In its glow we see things as they really are, not as they appear.

We see ourselves as kings and queens, priests and priestesses in the eyes of the Father. According to Greek legend, everything King Midas touched turned to gold. According to Christ, everything we touch is turned by our Father into a deed worthy of remembrance. He takes ten words of a servant girl and transforms a life forever. He takes our ten words, our ten patients, our ten classrooms, and transforms lives in his own way, in his own time. The God who created everything from nothing still uses his Word to create big out of little, a crown out of a cross.

All Saints' Day may be November 1, but it's also January 5 and March 15 and every other day on the calendar. Every day we remember to remember that we are never forgotten by our Father. We may feel lost in the winding pathways of a life that seems to be going nowhere, but that's God's favorite place to be. In Syria, scrubbing floors with a servant girl. In Mexico, sewing clothes in a factory. In Wisconsin, milking cows in a dairy. In Iowa, taking the Lord's Supper to an elderly shut-in. Backstage, with those who get no credit, Jesus is making much ado about the forgotten of the world.

His name we carry through every step, however faltering, we take on the journey through life. On our lips and in our hearts, let's walk to the beat of this beatitude: "Blessed are the anonymous, for they are named in the kingdom of God."

Discussion Questions

1. Talk about some examples of unfamous people and everyday vocations that we take for granted, that go overlooked. How are each of these a mask of God? How is God working through them? Discuss your own callings. How is the Lord using you?

_____

_____

_____

2. Read Revelation 7:9-10. Who does John see in Revelation 7? How are their robes made white (v. 14)? These people are called the saints, which just means "holy ones." Are all Christians saints? How is that title sometimes used as if there is a hierarchy of holiness in the church?

_____

_____

_____

3. Read Isaiah 49:14-16. Talk about loneliness and the feeling of being forgotten or overlooked. How does this affect a person? And how does Isaiah 49 speak to that? What do these verses say about the Lord's remembrance of his people: 1 Samuel 1:19; Psalm 25:6-7; Psalm 106:4.

_____

_____

_____

4. Talk about how anonymity can degenerate into a phobia. How does our culture of fame, social media influence, and bigger-is-better mentality fan the flames of this fear? Read Genesis 11:4. Why did the people want to build a tower? How did God respond to that tower and to our own "towers of Babel" today?

_____

_____

_____

5. Read Matthew 10:30 and Psalm 139:15-16. Discuss how these verses describe our Father's knowledge of us. What does such divine attention to detail tell us about God and his love toward us?

    _____

    _____

    _____

6. Read 1 Thessalonians 4:11; Matthew 6:3-4; Philippians 2:3; Romans 12:16; and Mark 9:35. Compare the outlook of all these passages with the mantras of modern society, such as "Second place is last place," "Stand out from the crowd," or "Be somebody." How do these biblical verses help us to understand humility, sacrifice, and love?

    _____

    _____

    _____

7. Review the account of Naaman and the "Jane Doe" servant girl in 2 Kings 5. Try to put yourself in her shoes. Contrast her position with that of her master. How did the Lord use this anonymous girl? What impact did this have on Naaman? How does this illumine the influence that our "little works" or "little lives" can have on others?

    _____

    _____

    _____

8. Talk about the many ways that numbers or statistics are used to measure us, justify us, or condemn us. When we try to exalt ourselves, how does the Lord respond? What does it mean that he "crucifies us" and how is this precisely the way that God joins us to Christ and assures us that we are never anonymous in his sight?

    _____

    _____

    _____

Seven

Unsexy Church

Several inches of fresh snow blanketed the half mile of frozen, impassable road that led from the house to the bus stop. The five of us walked along in a line, leaving a single set of huge tracks in the powder like one giant traveler was tramping through. We skirted half-finished, abandoned homes, now skeletal shadows in an otherwise white world. With each intake of breath, my burning lungs felt every digit of the -18 degrees that Sunday morning in January.

Siberia was living up to its reputation.

We took our seats on an unheated bus, sat in silence, and bounced along the streets of Novosibirsk, Russia's third largest city. Around 1.5 million people call this place home. One of them, years before, had begun questioning the atheism inculcated in him from infancy. He read the Bible and grappled with fundamental issues about God, himself, and the world in which he lived. Eventually he was baptized. A small group from the university gathered with him to study. Their numbers grew. In the mid-1990s, the leader of this small mission, Vsevolod Lytkin, became their pastor and they his flock. A few years later they even launched a small seminary, at which I was privileged to serve as guest lecturer.

The student beside me tapped me on the shoulder and pointed out the frosty window. "There's the church." I gazed up at a multistory gray apartment building that looked like the backdrop of a Soviet film. "This?" I asked. He smiled and nodded.

Once inside, we descended a flight of stairs into a damp basement abuzz with activity. Twenty or thirty people milled around. Babushkas in fur hats. Children eating gingerbread. Bearded men sipping tea. A deacon who spoke fluent English offered me a chair and asked me about my trip, the class I was teaching, and my family back in the States. I was halfway around the globe. But these fellow believers made me feel a little closer to home.

The other half of the basement served as the sanctuary. Up front stood a rectangular table draped in a plain white cloth. On top a silver chalice, a small plate, a Bible. A cross suspended on the wall behind it. A wooden stand for a pulpit. Folding chairs as pews.

The service began. I knew very little Russian, enough to be polite and ask simple questions. But their liturgy spoke in a language whose rhythms and cadence were in my blood. It was the same basic pattern followed by churches around the globe. Call and response, hymns and psalms, sermon and meal. Foreign words but the universal language of Jesus speaking grace into the lives of babushkas, little children, bearded old men, and this American far from home.

When worship ended, each of us walked back up that flight of stairs into the world, back to our daily lives. I to my teaching, others to hospitals, kitchens, factories. Yet each of us left enriched by the mystery of a kingdom encountered in a decidedly unregal place.

When my teaching stint was over, I boarded a plane that took me from Novosibirsk to Moscow to New York City, and eventually all 6,100 miles back to Oklahoma. Home sweet home. Here I served as the pastor of a small church in a town that didn't boast a single red light.

St. Paul's had been part of this rural community for one hundred years. In 1943, lightning struck the steeple and the flames slowly crawled from the top down. While bits of timber fell like burning rain, a band of courageous parishioners rushed inside to carry out the pews and altar. Four years later, when these faithful people rebuilt the church, the old furnishings found a new home.

The day after my return from Russia, I walked the two blocks from the parsonage to the church and pushed open the sanctuary door. For several minutes I just stood there, motionless in the silence, soaking in the familiar smells and sights of this sacred place. As I looked at those pews and the white altar, I reflected back on the hundred years of preaching, baptizing, singing, and communing in this place. If walls could talk, what stories these could tell.

Within a span of days, I had been inside two churches in two different cultures and continents. Though they were worlds apart, the two assemblies were born from the same womb. We spoke the same language of law and grace, repentance and faith, giving and thanksgiving. Russian boys and girls learned the same Lord's Prayer my children and I recited together while kneeling at the bedside every night. We confessed the same creeds. We were both contending "for the faith that was once for all delivered to the saints" (Jude 3).

We shared something else too. Neither church was the glamorous model that turns the heads of the world. More homely Leah than stunning Rachel. Simple spaces with an otherworldly allure. Beautiful, yes, but a beauty largely imperceptible to the eyes. Deeper, more profound. A kind of mystical simplicity. They didn't dress to impress but to conceal. And in that concealment, they revealed the "secret and hidden wisdom of God" (1 Cor. 2:7). The kind of wisdom learned in the classroom of the cross.

As I stood there in the sanctuary, looking around me, thinking back on where I'd been and where I now was, the ancient words of Jacob suddenly rose to my lips. I smiled and into the silence spoke this truth: "How awesome is this place! This is none other than the house of God, and this is the gate of heaven" (Gen. 28:17).

Holy Campground

The patriarch uttered that exclamation early one morning as he looked around the campground where he'd spent the night. On the surface it was an unexceptional place. A patch of soil with a few rocks strewn about, one of which he'd used for a pillow. Yet here he'd seen the unseen. A stairway bridging the gap between earth and heaven. Angels of God striding up and down the steps. And suddenly "the LORD was standing beside [Jacob]" (v. 13 JPS Tanakh). He spoke words of comfort to this man on the run. Confirmed ancient promises and made new ones. Assured him, "I am with you and will keep you wherever you go" (v. 15). When Jacob awoke, he said, "Surely the LORD is in this place, and I did not know it" (v. 16).

Of course he didn't know it. There was not a smidgen of the divine about it. No neon sign blinking the announcement "Hotel of God." Just dirt and rocks and unpromising darkness. Where no one would have guessed Yahweh was, there he revealed himself to a worn-down sinner in need of consolation. A young man with nothing to offer in return. One with a growing number of skeletons in his closet. Yet a sinner desperate for grace. The kind of undeserved gift that falls in our laps while we do nothing—indeed, can do nothing.

God stood in the dirt beside Jacob, bolstered his flagging confidence, and pledged his ongoing fidelity to this wayward child in a location that seemed to cradle no hope. That looked no more promising, in fact, than a certain hill outside Jerusalem where a Jewish rabbi was pierced by Roman nails. Yet here, as there, was the gate of heaven. Here was Bethel, the house of God. How awesome was this unawesome place.

Mi Casa Es Su Casa

God's homes throughout the centuries, from basements to basilicas, have all shared one thing in common: the only reason they're called God's house is because the Lord drove up in a U-Haul and moved in. His presence and his presence alone makes them heaven's earthly address. When Moses and his artisans finished the tabernacle, for example, the "glory of the LORD filled [it]" (Exod. 40:34). Later, on the day Solomon and his workers completed the temple, once more "the glory of the LORD filled the house of the LORD" (1 Kings 8:11). Likewise, when God's glory vacated the temple polluted by Israel's idolatry, it ceased to be the divine abode. It became just another piece of foreclosed real estate destined for the Babylonian bulldozer (Ezek. 10:18–19).

If God's not home, it's not God's home.

It's not much different now. True, gone are the days when we can point to the zip code and street address of an edifice in Jerusalem and say, "That's God's house." The Father's Son is now our tabernacle-in-the-flesh: "The Word became flesh and dwelt [literally, 'tabernacled'] among us, and we have seen his glory"

(John 1:14). Christ himself says he is the new temple, destroyed in crucifixion and reconstructed in three days (2:19). Paul describes our bodies as "temple[s] of the Holy Spirit" (1 Cor. 6:19) and Peter says we are like "living stones . . . being built up as a spiritual house" (1 Pet. 2:5). Despite these differences between the OT and NT, the essential truth remains: God's presence alone proclaims, "This is the house of God."

What we call "houses of God" today are concrete places where Christ is at home to do what he's always done. He lays aside his garments, takes a towel and basin of water, and washes the feet we've soiled on paths of disobedience. He cooks a meal and beckons us to take a seat at his table. He teaches us who we are, who he is, and who we become in him. He has us sing and pray and echo back to him what he's first said to us.

In other words, Christ works from home. Just as he came "not to be served but to serve, and to give his life as a ransom for many," so he sticks his head outside the church door and yells, "Come one, come all! I'm here to serve you with the fruits of the ransom I paid in full for you" (see Matt. 20:28). A church service is what Germans call *Gottesdienst*, God's service. It's not our service but his. He is there not only as Lord but as the Servant of his servants.

This entails something else as well: God's house is also the sinner's house. *Mi casa es su casa*, he says. My home is your home. Because of that, under the Lord's roof you'll always find quite a mess. Streaks of blood on the floor from the wounded who drag themselves there after a week on the battlefields of addiction, grief, and family disintegration. Scratches on the walls from those trying to claw their way free from demons within. Vomit on the carpet from women sick of abuse and men sick with anger. Overturned tables from infighting. Everywhere you look in the church are the shards of broken hearts, trails of tears, and the blank stares of God's children hungry for even a scrap of hope in a life racked by the famine of despair. We may be wearing a suit or blue jeans, a dress or shorts, but all of us who walk in the door of God's house are draped in filthy rags in need of whitening by the blood of the Lamb. In the church, cleanliness is not next to godliness; uncleanliness and ungodliness is all we have. And Jesus, over and over, purifies us with his blood.

This is comforting, to be sure, but also unsettling. In the sanctuary the grossness of our frailty, meanness, and evil is on full display. In the little congregation I served, for instance, only about seventy-five people gathered on Sunday mornings. Among them was the alcoholic who showed up, more than once, on a congregational workday to cuss out our trustees for spending too much money. Two elderly women still feuding over suspicions of a husband's infidelity from thirty years before. The couple who regularly dialed 9-1-1 to report domestic abuse. The porn addict. The serial divorcée. The rumormonger. The church of God is also the house of human failures.

That tiny Oklahoma congregation was a microcosm of broken humanity. A living monument to how evil takes a chain saw to lives, marriages, and friendships.

Yet there we were, Sunday after Sunday, elbow to elbow in the same sanctuary, bathed in the same baptismal font, drinking from the same cup, hearing from the same Bible, members of the same body of Jesus. This flock might at times have resembled more a pack of mangy wolves, but the Lamb of God stood steadfast and immovable in our midst, taking away the sins of the world—including ours.

Whether God's house is underground in Siberia, a clapboard house in an Ohio cornfield, or the Washington National Cathedral, they are all the chosen communities where the Holy Spirit, living among us unholy sinners, is hard at work. In quiet and slow and unassuming ways, he is transforming us into the image of the Father's Son.

It's these quiet and slow and unassuming ways, however, that prove to be one of the hardest truths for us to swallow.

The Season of the Flat Tire

Around the first of December this past year, my pastor stepped into the pulpit to begin a sermon purposely designed to drive us mad with impatience. We had just transitioned into that four-week season of the church year called Advent, but which I have nicknamed the Season of the Flat Tire.

As we're rocketing along the interstate of our lives, scrambling from appointment to appointment, ticking off items on our to-do list, God shoves a huge nail in one of our tires. In an instant, the rubber flies. We limp over to the guardrail and there we sit. Stranded, frustrated, probably uttering a few choice words about this delay. We've got places to go and things to do, especially in these weeks leading up to Christmas. But we're going nowhere fast now. The world continues to buzz on by, but the church is disabled on the side of the road. Now all we can do is hurry up and wait. Our progress is arrested, our rabbit lives forced into a turtle's pace.

Welcome to the flat tire of Advent.

For about twenty-five days, the New Testament church walks a mile in Old Testament shoes. Advent means "coming" or "arrival." During this season, we are Abraham and Sarah, waiting one hundred years and ninety years, respectively, for the advent of baby Isaac. We are Israel, dragging our feet for forty years through the desert sands of Sinai until our arrival at the land flowing with milk and honey. We are David on the run, forced to wait, year after year, until Saul's death, when we finally mount the throne God has prepared for us. There's no speeding up Advent. All we can do is twiddle our thumbs. The air's out of our tire. God is making us wait.

In that Sunday sermon, our pastor opened his Bible to the first chapter of Matthew. He began to read. "The book of the genealogy of Jesus, the son of David, the son of Abraham . . ." He paused, glanced up at our questioning faces, and continued to read. "Abraham was the father of Isaac, and Isaac was the father of Jacob, and Jacob was the father of Judah and his brothers . . ." On and on he read. Verse after verse. Name after oddball name. For what seemed an hour, he subjected us to this interminable, dry, boring litany. Halfway through, I leaned over to my wife and whispered, "Is this ever going to end?"

And finally it did. He finished naming the last twig on Jesus's family tree. He closed the Bible. And as he began to preach, we learned a valuable lesson about the quiet, slow, unassuming ways our Lord has always labored in his church.

God promised to send the Messiah immediately after sin slithered into our world (Gen. 3:15). The seed of the woman would crush the head of the serpent. We might suppose, as Adam and Eve likely did, that God would do this sooner rather than later. Why wait? In fact, it's possible that Eve reckoned her firstborn son, Cain, to be this promised savior. The Hebrew of Genesis 4:1 can be translated "Now Adam knew his wife, and she conceived and bore Cain, saying, 'I have gotten a man, the LORD.'"[1] She was wrong, of course, dreadfully wrong, since this child was anything but the Lord. He grew up to be a murderer, not a messiah. But I can respect her eagerness, her fervent hope that God would expedite our salvation. She and her husband had made a mess of our virgin world. They hoped the Lord would intervene swiftly and decisively to make it pristine again.

Little did this first mother know it wouldn't be years, or even decades or centuries, before God would make good on his promise. It would be millennia. The Lord would make us sit in the waiting room. A child would be conceived and born. Was this the Messiah? No. Another child would be conceived and born. Was this the Messiah? No, again. So-and-so begat so-and-so begat so-and-so as the centuries crept toward Bethlehem.

Through the quiet, slow, unassuming process of conception, gestation, and diaper changing, God was subjecting his people to a highly unpopular timetable—a slow one. "One day is as a thousand years" to the Lord, and "a thousand years as one day" (2 Pet. 3:8). He is "not slow to fulfill his promise as some count slowness, but is patient toward you, not wishing that any should perish, but that all should reach repentance" (v. 9). I chuckle every time I read those words: "as some count slowness." Like there's anyone who really thinks that waiting millennia for the first coming of Jesus, and more millennia for his second coming, is not slow. Hurry up, God!

But you won't find a lead-footed Jesus barreling around a NASCAR race-track. He rarely gets out of granny gear. In fact, he seems to get a thrill out of flat tires. So in his kingdom, if you think things are going to be fast-paced, with a goose-pimpled, adrenaline-drunk, razzle-dazzle craziness about them, you're in for the shock of your life.

The work of Jesus in our lives, and in the life of his church, creeps along like that Matthew genealogy. It's not radical, explosive, immediate, incredible, or any other dazzling adjective you can select from the *Thesaurus of Spiritual Excitement*. There's no microwaving this sacred meal. It's going to take time. It's going to be humdrum most of the time. Worship won't be an ongoing string of wow! mind-blowing! incredible! experiences that leave us tingling with the skin-tight closeness of the Spirit.

Jesus is more of a take-his-sweet-time gardener than an applause-inducing circus performer. Novelty is not his way. We often want it to be. Indeed, as the devil Screwtape brags in one of his letters to the junior tempter, "The horror of the Same Old Thing is one of the most valuable passions we have produced in the human heart."[2] Unsatisfied with the built-in rhythms of change in daily life, "the horror of the Same Old Thing" demands novelty for novelty's sake. "Unchanged" comes to mean "stagnant."[3]

But think *advent*, not adrenaline, when you picture life in Christ's church. Sure, sometimes there are emotional highs during worship. Page through the Bible and you'll read about some of these as well. At that first Christian Pentecost, for instance, when the Spirit swooped down and appeared like tongues of fire dancing atop the heads of the disciples, people were awestruck with wonder. This was certainly novel.

But what about the following Lord's Day when no tongues of fire appeared, just regular human tongues reading and speaking the Spirit's Word? Or the Sundays after that? The Spirit hadn't gone on vacation or lost his voice. He was there, doing his ordinary, unchanging work. He was at home among his people, laboring without hurry, without fanfare, without bells and whistles, to give the fruits of Jesus to hungry people, to transform them by the renewing of their minds, to shepherd the shepherds as they led the lambs of Christ by his Word. He was doing then what he continues to do now.

The Next Big Thing vs. the Old Little Things

When we're always on the lookout for the next big thing that God is doing in the church, we grow blind to the old little things he's been doing all along. He's a genealogy kind of Messiah. Easing us along, working slowly and often imperceptibly in our lives and congregations in his quiet and unobtrusive ways. His transformative acts among us will likely never even register on our mental radar.

Subtle, not scintillating—that's the watchword of the sanctifying work of the Spirit in his church.

He is, for instance, teaching us the language of heaven in his earthly house. Even in the womb, children hear the voices of their fathers and mothers. When they're born, and as they mature from infants to toddlers to teenagers to adults, the words of their parents shape them, teach them.

English is my native language. I don't remember learning it. It simply became part of me as I grew up. Through the slow, steady, daily absorption of English, I learned words, grammar, structure. This particular language forms my understanding of the world, myself, my neighbors—my sense of time, importance, and so much more. Yet there was no big, exciting day when, in a flash of illumination, I swallowed the language whole and began speaking it.

Our Father teaches us the language of heaven in the same way. Paul urges Timothy to "follow the pattern of the sound words that you have heard from me" (2 Tim. 1:13). He began learning this "pattern of sound words" already in childhood, for "from infancy" he had known "the Holy Scriptures" (3:15 NIV). When we gather together as the body of Christ, his Word reverberates through the sanctuary in readings, prayers, psalms, hymns, creeds, and sermons. And, like children, we imitate the speech of our Abba. We echo back to him what he first says to us. He teaches us to pray, "Our Father in heaven" (Matt. 6:9). He teaches us to chant, "The LORD is my shepherd; I shall not want" (Ps. 23:1). He teaches us to confess, "If we say we have no sin, we deceive ourselves, and the truth is not in us. If we confess our sins, he is faithful and just to forgive us our sins and to cleanse us from all unrighteousness" (1 John 1:8–9). He teaches us the language of his table, "This is my body, which is for you. . . . This cup is the new covenant in my blood" (1 Cor. 11:24–25).

The sanctuary becomes one big swimming pool of the Spirit's verbal waters. We dive in. They soak us through and through. And over time, this language shapes our view of God, ourselves, and the world, as all language does. Speaking of the Lord's Prayer, Jen Pollock Michel urges that as we say these words, we are "immersing ourselves in Jesus's language," so that "our hearts realign with God's purposes and priorities."[4] Rather than being conformed to this world—to its language of power, self-determination, and the narcissistic demand for immediate gratification—we are "transformed by the renewal of [our] mind" (Rom. 12:2). The Spirit gives us "the mind of Christ" (1 Cor. 2:16).

Through his scalpel, this divine surgeon also removes "the heart of stone . . . and give[s] you a heart of flesh" (Ezek. 36:26). A new heart beating with new loves. The love of God, the love of neighbor, the love that "bears all things, believes all things, hopes all things, endures all things" (1 Cor. 13:7). In his book *You Are What You Love*, James K. A. Smith explores in depth how, in worship, the Spirit recalibrates our hearts through "love-shaping liturgies" to desire the good life God intends for us.[5] "To be human," he writes, "is to be a liturgical animal, a creature whose loves are shaped by our worship."[6] Through the cultivation of habits in worship, Christ is reshaping our hearts to be in conformity with his own.

All this doesn't happen in a flash, of course. It happens slowly and without pageantry. It happens when we stop insisting that the Spirit hurry up and do something that'll leave us perched on the edge of our seats. It happens when we sober up from our addiction to immediacy. "Hurry up!" is not in our Lord's vocabulary. He's not out to stimulate us with titillating episodes of divine entertainment. In little ways, over long periods of time, with the patience of eternity, he's re-creating us by his Word, in his church, to walk out the doors of the sanctuary, bearing on our lips the language of light to speak into a world choking in darkness.

The Old, Old Story

When I got back from my trip to Siberia, I found heaped atop my desk the mail that had accumulated during my absence. Mixed in with the pile of letters and bills were several glossy pamphlets from various organizations that offered products to congregations. One promised, "Attend this seminar to revolutionize your ministry!" Another advertised, "Read this book to revitalize your congregation!"

The subtext of every one of them was the same: what you're doing now is not enough. Not exciting enough. Not relevant enough. Not revolutionary enough. The time has come to re-create and refine the church's dull image. What she desperately needs to do is sexy herself up.

What the church desperately needs, however, is not the ecclesiastical equivalent of a boob job and a membership at Gold's Gym. She needs more flat tires. More genealogy sermons. More trips to Siberian basements and pilgrimages to rural congregations where the good news of Christ crucified and risen for you reverberates through the sanctuary, shapes youth events, molds VBS programs, and floods the pastor's sermons. As Michael Horton writes, "In the church today, we do not need more conferences, more programs, and more celebrities. We need more churches where the Spirit is immersing sinners into Christ day by day, a living communion of the saints, where we cannot simply jump to our favorite chapter or Google our momentary interest."[7] What the church needs is a bold and unapologetic return to—what the hymn calls—the "old, old story of Jesus and his love."[8] That heart of love, palpitating with crucifixion mercy, is the touchstone of every congregational action. And the gospel is always more than enough. It is everything.

The church doesn't need a new thing; it needs the ancient gifts reaffirmed, reembraced, and preached as "the power of God for salvation to everyone who believes" (Rom. 1:16). The good news of the God who walked about not as a superhero but an ordinary man, who hung out with the immoral riffraff the über-religious shunned, who declared helpless children the greatest in the kingdom, and who manifested his glory in the gory epiphany of the cross.

The Mega of Megachurches

The push for "more" in worship—more Hollywood-esque drama, more emotional experiences, more sports-arena spectacle—is a direct result of less awareness of what's really happening as the church gathers. By and large, we've forgotten that when the church gathers around the gifts of Jesus, precisely there is heaven on earth. The base of Jacob's ladder rests in the middle of the church's sanctuary.

Every gathered family of God, whether they meet in a living room, a mud hut, or a towering cathedral, has one thing in common: more worshipers are present than meets the eye. In the Sunday bulletin in my congregation, there's a worship attendance number. But it's always wrong, a gross underestimation. No usher can stand in the balcony and tally up those present in the sanctuary.

Even in mini-churches the mega of megachurches is concealed: the one, holy, Christian, and apostolic church.

When the Spirit summons us from the daily grind of our Monday–Saturday lives to circle round pulpits and altars and baptismal waters, we step into a hidden reality that is more vast than any of us can fathom. Like Jacob, what we suppose is a common place ends up being the very portal of heaven. For where Jesus is, there his whole church is. And where Jesus is, there his angels and archangels are. And where Jesus is, there is the Father and the Holy Spirit.

Where our Lord embraces his bride with mercy and grace, all of heaven crashes the party.

No eye can see, no mind perceive, the throng squeezed within the four walls of any structure housing sinners Jesus has come to serve. Whole companies of cherubim perch atop the rafters, peering down upon those they are called to protect. Tens of thousands of seraphim wing their way, like flocks of birds, round and round the altar. Saints who have left this vale of tears, who have entered paradise with Jesus, accompany him to a grand reunion with those of us who still work and weep our way through life. It's standing room only in every church, whether ten or ten thousand are visible. For invisibly present are the innumerable company of angels, archangels, and all the saints of heaven. Every Sunday is a little taste of what our eyes will finally behold in the resurrection on the last day.

John saw this in Revelation "on the Lord's day" (Rev. 1:10). He beheld "a door standing open in heaven" (4:1). And inside that door he saw what we don't see but is nevertheless present: thrones, living creatures, saints in white—the Lamb who was slain, worthy to "receive power and wealth and wisdom and might and honor and glory and blessing" (5:12).

Isaiah beheld this in Jerusalem when he "saw the Lord sitting upon a throne, high and lifted up; and the train of his robe filled the temple" (Isa. 6:1). A choir of six-winged seraphim flew about the sanctuary, chanting, "Holy, holy, holy is the LORD of hosts; the whole earth is full of his glory!" (v. 3). The foundations shook. Smoke of incense clouded the house. Isaiah saw through the earthly veil of the Jerusalem temple to the heavenly reality of what was really happening in the daily worship of the Israelites.

In worship, the church doesn't imitate below what happens above. We participate in it. We all show up late for church. The service has already begun by the time we park our vehicles and walk inside. The praise around the throne of the Lamb is ongoing. And when we leave church, the service continues. For an hour or so,

[We] have come to Mount Zion and to the city of the living God, the heavenly Jerusalem, and to innumerable angels in festal gathering, and to the assembly of the firstborn who are enrolled in heaven, and to God, the judge of all, and to the spirits of the righteous made perfect, and to Jesus, the mediator of a new covenant, and to the sprinkled blood that speaks a better word than the blood of Abel. (Heb. 12:22–24)

Notice that the preacher in Hebrews does not say we *will* come to this place but we *have* come to this place. We come there every Lord's Day, in congregations large and small, rustic and resplendent, in Siberia and Oklahoma. We all meet at the peak of Mount Zion.

Unawareness of this hidden reality breeds a dissatisfaction with the plain old stuff we see around us. But this plain old stuff is suffused with sanctity. The cup on the altar is full of wine that fermented in the veins of God. The font splashes with water that spilled from the spear-pierced side of Jesus. The pulpit is the open mouth of the Spirit. These plumbers and accountants and first-graders around us have been crowned as kings and queens in the kingdom of God. The minister who's never stepped foot inside a gym, who hasn't a single tattoo, who tells corny jokes—when he preaches the Lord's law and gospel, when he pours baptismal water over the heads of sinners, when he says, "I forgive you in the name of the Father and of the Son and of the Holy Spirit," then he is on par with Moses, Elijah, and Paul, a chosen ambassador of the almighty God.

This plain old stuff, these plain old people, are God's stuff, God's people. And as such they wear the plain garb of the cross on which God made his ultimate revelation. Luther reminds us, "It is not the stones, the construction, and the gorgeous silver and gold that make a church beautiful and holy."[9] What is it, then?

> It is the Word of God and sound preaching. For where the goodness of God is commended to men and hearts are encouraged to put their trust in Him and to call upon God in danger, there is truly a holy church. Whether it is in a dark nook or a bare hill or a barren tree, it is truthfully and correctly called a house of God and a gate of heaven, even though it is without a roof, under the clouds and open sky.[10]

Wherever we gather with our brothers and sisters in Christ around his Word, be it as unattractive as a basement, as simple as a country chapel, or as remote as a military tent in a war zone, there is Bethel. There is Christ standing beside us. There, in his quiet, slow, unassuming ways, he's pouring abnormal grace into us normal people who are royalty in the kingdom of heaven.

Discussion Questions

1. This chapter described two churches, one in Siberia and one in Oklahoma. Though externally they were different, what did they share in common? While we tend to focus on the differences between churches, what are some of the truths, practices, and traditions they share in common?

   _____

   _____

   _____

2. Read Genesis 28:10-22. Why was Jacob surprised to discover that his campground was the "house of God" and "gate of heaven"? In what ways are churches like (or unlike) that campground?

   _____

   _____

   _____

3. Discuss God's various "homes" in the Bible, from the tabernacle, to the temple, to Jesus and his church. Use these passages to trace the web of connections between the various "homes": Exodus 40:34, 1 Kings 8:11, John 1:14, John 2:19, 1 Corinthians 6:19, and 1 Peter 2:5.

   _____

   _____

   _____

4. Talk about the meaning of a "church service." Service entails someone serving and someone being served. If we think of worship as primarily where Christ serves us, how does that change our perspective on the reason we gather as the church (Matthew 20:28)? Discuss the examples of how this service is both comforting but also unsettling.

   _____

   _____

   _____

5. In the section, "The Season of the Flat Tire," reference is made to Matthew 1:1-17. Scan that genealogy. What does this long list teach us about God's ways? His promises? The speed at which he works? What is "the horror of the same old thing" and how do you see that play out in your own life as well as the life of the church?

_____

_____

_____

6. What is meant by the "language of heaven" and how is this language taught at home and in church? How do these verses contribute to the discussion: Matthew 6:9-13; Acts 2:42; and 2 Timothy 3:14-17?

_____

_____

_____

7. What distracts the church from focusing on the "old, old story of Jesus and his love"? How can we return to—or remain at—the primary focus of keeping Christ and his Gospel front and center?

_____

_____

_____

8. Read Hebrews 12:22-24. Talk about how this is a description of what happens every time the church gathers for worship. What does this teach us about the unseen realities around the worshiping people of God? How does this enrich our understanding of what happens on Sunday morning?

_____

_____

_____

Eight

Learning about God
in the Devil's Classroom

We were ripping away crumbling shingles and rotting plywood from the roof of a paper mill in northern Indiana. The July sun baking us brown. I was a seminary student making a little cash during the summer break. Mark was head honcho of the roofing crew. He was a shrimp of a man whose family had been shunned from an Amish community back in the '80s for owning a boom box. At least that's the tale he told. Every day, he and I, along with a giant nicknamed Possum and a chain-smoker named Keith, would shinny up the ladder and break our backs to earn a buck.

Mark was my professor that summer. He taught me how to lay shingles out straight as shafts of light, fit flashing around chimneys to prevent leaks, and fire a nail gun like a pro. In our daily conversations, he also recounted stories of what community life had been like among a people who still rode in buggies and used horses to plow their fields. An ex-Amish teacher schooled this future Lutheran minister on the fine art of keeping the occupants of a house nice and dry, as well as what it was like to live inside a home lacking most of the creature comforts we take for granted.

A couple of summers earlier, I was working in the woodshop of a university maintenance department in Austin, Texas. Alongside me sat a man in a wheelchair. Years before, a motorcycle accident had left Fred paralyzed from the waist down. But his spirit was far from disabled. He was one of those rare men who always rolled into work, even on Mondays, with a smile beaming from his face. When he wasn't sawing lumber, he was strumming tunes on his guitar. In fact, so extraordinary were his musical talents that he was even recognized by legendary country music star George Strait, who included a song by Fred on one of his many platinum albums.[1]

That summer Fred was my professor. He taught me how to make a variety of cuts with a Skilsaw, guided my complete reconstruction of a dilapidated office desk, and introduced me to the intricate art of crafting dovetail joints. In this classroom clouded with sawdust, I acquired skills I've used over the last twenty-five years to build everything from bookshelves to a food pantry for my mother's kitchen. This musical man in a wheelchair stands tall in my memory. He taught me not only how to work with lumber but how to work with life, especially when the life you once knew was fundamentally altered.

I suppose most of us have had a few unusual teachers. Talented men and women with backstories that set them apart. They guide our hands and shape our outlooks, passing along skills that often extend beyond the practical. Mark the roofer introduced me to the ethos of the Amish world he'd left behind. Fred the carpenter introduced me to a life lived in joyful surrender to a cross he didn't choose.

Over the years, throughout my twenties and thirties, I had scores of other teachers. I sat at the feet of brilliant academic minds. An MIT grad guided me through the labyrinthine paths of the Hebrew verbal system. I learned to swim in the sea of the Talmud with rabbis at Hebrew Union College. Still others immersed me in the philosophical and theological arguments of everyone from Philo to Luther to Kant to Barth. I had three master's degrees under my belt by the time I wrapped up my studies. And eventually I fell so head-over-heels for the academy that I myself became part of it as a professor of Hebrew and the Old Testament.

From all these Jewish and Christian teachers I learned much about God. In fact, you might say I learned too much.

Before my senior year in college, I traveled with a university biology class to the Grand Canyon. We hiked the seven miles of winding trails descending from the rim to the canyon floor. Once there, we pitched our tents alongside Bright Angel Creek. A beautiful, hidden paradise. On either side of these flowing waters lush vegetation grows. But shift a few feet away from the creek and you cross an invisible threshold into arid desert dust where nothing but cacti grow. Two ecosystems sit side-by-side, one full, one empty. One wet, another bone dry.

That was me in the academy. A man hosting two interior ecosystems. The theological rivers flowed only through the hemispheres in my brain, leaving my heart and life as dry as Grand Canyon dirt. I'd erected a dam between my brain and the rest of me. I learned much about God—too much, because it was all cerebral stuff. I had morphed into a talking head of theology. A professional religionist.

Our Father, seeing my condition, knew his wayward child needed a novel kind of teacher. An unusual professor. So he sent an explosives expert into my life. One who planted dynamite at the base of my cerebral dam. The blast sent theological and biblical waters rolling down to inundate the arid regions of my body and life. Unbeknownst to me at the time, the Lord had enrolled me in the school of this instructor.

Like untold others through the centuries, including many in ancient Israel, I became a student in the devil's classroom.

Joseph: When Dreams Become Nightmares

Scrawled on one of the old desks in this classroom you'll discover, barely visible, the words "Joseph was here." Not for four years, or even eight, but for thirteen years this favorite son of Jacob was enrolled in the academy of suffering. From age seventeen to thirty, Joseph learned that theology is taught not only in books but in waterless pits, lustful bedrooms, dark dungeons, back-stabbing brothers, and promise-breaking friends—in people and places the devil likes to use.

At some point on our pilgrimage through this world, we walk a mile or two in Joseph's shoes. Sometimes many more. The bottom falls out of our lives. It might be the loss of a job or career, the decimation of marriage, the burial of a child, a paralyzing accident like the one that befell my friend Fred. Or it might happen slowly, almost imperceptibly. One day we wake up to realize we've let all our loves wither away. We hate going to work. We hate looking in the mirror. We hate everything. Or we're so exhausted we can't even muster up hate. We just exist. A meaningless blob of humanity oozing its way toward the grave. We wonder why God even wasted his time creating us.

What fears and regrets and anxieties crippled Joseph during those thirteen years? His brothers sold him into bondage for chump change, the jilted wife of his master falsely accused him of trying to bed her, his fellow convict conveniently "forgot" to return a favor when he walked free. As a teenager, God had filled Joseph's dreams with vistas of greatness. His father, mother, and siblings bowing down to him. But now he sat in the dirt, bowed down by the weight of wasted years and rusting dreams.

A psalm about Joseph says, "His feet were hurt with fetters; his neck was put in a collar of iron" (Ps. 105:18). The music of freedom was replaced by the clanging of shackles with every step. The skin of his neck chafed raw by the collar of iron. And, while all this was happening, where were you, God? What happened to the almighty dream-giver of his youth? Was that all a malicious phantom of his juvenile imagination? Had you wadded Joseph up like a piece of garbage and tossed him into the Egyptian dump?

When you're a student in the classroom of the devil, such interrogations of heaven rise like bile from the pit of your stomach. You forget the polite prayer etiquette you learned in Sunday school. You stand outside the barred door of God's secret counsel and bang your fist bloody on the wood, demanding entrance, demanding answers, demanding that God sit down with you face-to-face and explain himself. But the only sound reaching your ears is the roar of silence. Scream as many prayers toward heaven as you wish. They all ricochet off and echo back to earth.

This wasn't the way Joseph's life was supposed to pan out. And this isn't the way our life of faith is supposed to go, either. Where's the so-called victorious Christian life? Where's all the glory? Something's gone terribly wrong. This God doesn't fit into the box of happy, glorious, smiling Christianity that is so popular in many American pulpits.

As we sit alongside Joseph in his cell, the Lord comes across as hard and mean and frigid. Like chunks of arctic ice float in his heart. Like he doesn't care if we're dead or alive, healthy or sick. God feels more like that distant uncle we've heard ugly stories about than a Father of grace and mercy.

The day finally came when Joseph was ushered out of the prison's tomb, had a shower and shave, and stood before Pharaoh. He went from being a prisoner to a potentate, elevated to the king's right hand. It was his own personal Easter. The day of resurrection after a thirteen-year Good Friday.

The psalm continues, "Until what he had said came to pass, the word of the LORD tested him" (v. 19). Until. Now it begins to some make sense. God was testing and trying Joseph until his time came. Reshaping the youthful dreamer into a mature man, seasoned by suffering, made wise by pain that he might "teach his elders wisdom" (v. 22).

Joseph graduated from the classroom of the devil with a PhD in the theology of the cross. He learned—and teaches us still—that the spiritual life is not about our own inner strength but the outward might of God. That we look not to ourselves but to the One who's promised to abide with us, even when he seems galaxies away.

Joseph came to realize one of the most important truths about God: not our outward circumstances, not our emotions or anxieties, but the Word of God alone dictates truth. And that Word promises that the Lord who seems so distant actually sits beside us in our prisons, lies with us on our hospital beds, and kneels with us in the dirt beside the graves of our children. Far from abandoning us as we bear our crosses, he presses us ever more deeply into his own crucified flesh and blood, grafting us to his skin, uniting us with himself so our identities are subsumed into his.

We are never closer to God than when we feel he's farthest away.

The Devil's Classes on Freedom, Pleasure, Independence

In one of his table talks, Martin Luther said,

> I did not learn my theology all at once, but had to search constantly deeper and deeper for it. My temptations did that for me, for no one can understand Holy Scripture without practice and temptations. This is what the enthusiasts and sects lack. *They don't have the right critic, the devil, who is the best teacher of theology.* If we don't have that kind of devil, then we become nothing but speculative theologians, who do nothing but walk around in our own thoughts and speculate with our reason alone as to whether things should be like this, or like that.[2]

The devil became my teacher of theology when I was a teacher of theology myself. But I had devolved into one of those fools whom Luther lambasts. A speculative theologian who walks about enamored with his own thoughts. And the orbit of my own thoughts increasingly revolved around the sun of my ego. My trophies. My accolades. And my carnal desires. I have recounted the whole journey in my book *Night Driving: Notes from a Prodigal Soul*.[3] I slouched into the gutter of lust and infidelity. I wrecked my marriage, job, career, and reputation. Took one step forward into a second hasty marriage, then two steps back into a subsequent divorce. Found myself hating God, cursing his very existence, and wishing—even praying through gritted teeth—that he would send a bolt of lightning to burn my already meaningless life to a heap of ashes.

I didn't know it at the time, but Christ had forced the devil to be my professor. He was God's tool to teach me what happens when my will is done. I took Satan's course on Freedom 101. And there I learned how thick the walls were in the prisons of perversion I made for myself. While taking his class on Pleasure, I learned how to drink my tears and lick my wounds and rip open prettily wrapped presents full of nothing but vapor and smoke. And I sat through several semesters of his course on Independence, where the devil showed me that I was a slave of a corrupt will and base desires, that every intention of the thoughts of my heart was only evil continually (Gen. 6:5). I racked up credit after credit in this university of iniquity. Failure was the only passing grade. Each semester brought me lower and lower until my hardening heart hit rock bottom and shattered. Only when I was reduced to nothing and confessed that I was a walking corpse was I ready for graduation.

When you leave the devil's classroom, you don't walk across a stage, chest puffed out with a new sense of self-worth, beaming as you receive your diploma. You're carried out in a coffin. Then, and only then, are you fit material for the work of our Lord. You have to be dead to yourself to be resurrected in Jesus.

Count Your Blessings or Your Crosses?

In the Baptist church of my youth, one of our go-to hymns was "Count Your Blessings." When you're tossed about by the tempests of life, the poet says, when you think everything is lost and the burden of your cross seems too heavy to bear, then:

> Count your blessings, name them one by one;
> Count your blessings, see what God hath done;
> Count your blessings, name them one by one,
> Count your many blessings, see what God hath done.[4]

Over the years, I came to realize that counting your blessings is not nearly as easy as picking up pen and paper and making a list. Sure, we can confidently number many good gifts in our lives: spouses, children, friends. But if we kept a spiritual scrapbook of "God's Blessings," there are many life pictures we'd be loath to paste.

Our typical litmus test that determines whether or not something is a blessing is this: Does it make us happy? If it makes us smile, it's a blessing. If it makes our lives a little easier, elevates us on the social scale, or simply makes us feel better about ourselves, then it qualifies as a blessing.

On the other hand, if something multiplies problems in our lives, makes us question our ability to maintain control of a situation, sullies our reputation, leads to heightened stress, or generally makes us feel worse about ourselves, then it's no blessing. We may not label it a curse, but it's certainly not something we're going to humblebrag about on Facebook.

If there's anything we've learned in these chapters, however, it's that our Father's blessings are not as easy to spot as brightly wrapped, bow-tied packages under the Christmas tree. They're often covered in brown paper under the bloody tree of the cross. They often don't seem good at all but burdensome, perhaps even defeating. Such "blessings" look like a burned-out bridge on the highway to our personal happiness.

This is an invaluable truth learned in the classroom of the devil: that trials and temptations, burdens and losses, are where God is most active to bring his grace into our lives. Counting your blessings includes counting your crosses, for Christ is hidden in suffering to lead us toward the blessings he desires for us.

Joseph beheld this truth with the clarity that only comes from post-Easter vision. He said to his brothers, "As for you, you meant evil against me, but God meant it for good, to bring it about that many people should be kept alive, as they are today" (Gen. 50:20). In my own experience, I later realized that I meant evil against myself, but God let me plummet into rebellion, and finally into the grave of defeat, to bring it about that I should be made alive again.

The Lord doesn't want us to realize how good we are, to tap into some inner strength. He wants us to confess that from conception we are navel-gazing, self-concerned rebels who look out for number one (Ps. 51:5). Rather than looking within ourselves to see the spark of true greatness, we are bid by God to peer into our hearts and realize that they are cardiac coffins, "deceitful above all things, and desperately sick" (Jer. 17:9). That even our glowing works, the religious acts we deem worthy of a plaque on heaven's wall, are the righteousness that Isaiah labels "a polluted garment" (Isa. 64:6). We don't need pep talks from the Spirit or self-help books that preach the false gospel of "God helps those who help themselves." We need to die to ourselves, to bleed into the grave with Christ, and to be raised to newness of life in his resurrection.

What doesn't kill you only prevents Easter from happening.

We balk at all this, of course, because we all want a life free of cares and concerns and crosses. So the Lord is constantly overhauling the engines of our hearts and minds. The Spirit gives us a new set of eyes to see that divine work often appears like the devil's work. Because these are often one and the same. The devil is no free agent, able to wreak havoc across the globe willy-nilly. Like sin and death, the devil is under God's thumb. He can't touch a hair of our heads without the Lord's nod. So Christ uses him—as he can use any evil—for good. When this is happening, few of us realize it. We're too short-sighted. But that's okay. We have a long-sighted Lord who's the Superintendent of the school in which the devil teaches. And many are his students, including a certain weak, strong man from the epoch of Israel's judges.

Samson: The Strongest, Weakest Man

Samson was the strongest of men. When a lion attacked him, he "tore [it] in pieces as one tears a young goat" (Judg. 14:6). He laid waste to a thousand Philistines with the jawbone of a donkey (15:15). And he lifted a city gate from its foundations and heaved it to the top of a hill (16:3). Had there been a World's Strongest Man competition in the ancient world, he'd have worn the crown for years. His strength was not in his biceps, however, but was God's gift, given by the Spirit's power.

And Samson was the weakest of men. He lived in a time when "everyone did what was right in his own eyes" (17:6). In that respect, Samson didn't seem much different from his contemporaries. When he wasn't shedding blood or burning crops, he was chasing skirts. Lots of them. He said he wanted to marry a girl—a Philistine—because "she looks good to me" (14:3 NASB). He paid for the services of a prostitute in the town of Gaza (16:1–3). And then there was his well-known lover, Delilah, who with her lying words and sharpened scissors finally brought Samson to his knees (vv. 4–22). The Philistines captured him, gouged out his eyes, and led him away in shackles.

This incarnation of testosterone was now a hairless, eyeless grunt of a slave. Nothing to strike terror in the hearts of his foes now. He was ruined. A laughing-stock for the Philistines. A plaything for the enemies of God to mock. Samson had been a student in the devil's classroom off and on throughout his life. Now he was there 24/7, reading, like Braille, the textbooks on humility and repentance.

We may find it hard to see ourselves in Samson, but we're more his spiritual doppelgangers than we realize—or perhaps care to admit. Broken by our failures, groping about for happiness in all the wrong places, flirting with hopelessness, many of us incarcerated in dungeons of addiction. We've all been there—or likely will be at some point in our lives. Even if we're fortunate enough to be spared some of the worst, someone we love won't be. Our parent, our spouse, our child or close friend will be that Samson. And we will be called to love them by bearing their burdens with them, by becoming their co-sufferer.

When that happens, during those most trying times in life, we need more than the shallow self-help spirituality that often masquerades as biblical faith. We don't need a message that says, "Be optimistic, focus on personal power, name and claim your best life now, see inside yourselves the strength to overcome." We also need more than a divine cheerleader who shouts encouragement from the sidelines of suffering. Who says, "You got this. I believe in you. You can do it!"

We need grace that invades our life from the outside, that floods graves with vitality, despair with hope. We need the Savior who crawls into the pit with us, takes us broken and bleeding in his arms, and bears us home to his Father's house.

In the loss of all things, we find the God of all grace, who gives us all things in his Son. He gives us the one in whom "the whole fullness of the deity dwells bodily" (Col. 2:9). The one who, in that same divine body, was broken on the cross for us.

So he did with our friend, Samson, who accomplished his greatest victory only when he had been weakened by the cross of suffering. While three thousand Philistines entertained themselves by thumbing their nose at him, Samson brought the house down—literally. He prayed one last prayer, pushed down the pillars of the idol temple, and buried more of his enemies in the rubble than he'd slain in his lifetime (Judg. 16:30). Hebrews numbers Samson among those who, by faith, "were made strong out of weakness" (Heb. 11:34). Finally emptied of himself, he was the ideal receptacle for the strength of the Lord. A student in the classroom of the devil, having passed through the most extreme of trials, he graduated *magna cum laude*.

Uncomfortable Christianity

For the rest of us, school is still in session. The temptations wax and wane, but they never go away. The heft of our crosses varies from year to year, sometimes day to day, but all Christians walk about with some wood crisscrossing their backs. "If anyone would come after me," Jesus said, "let him deny himself and take up his cross and follow me" (Matt. 16:24). He goes on, "For whoever would save his life will lose it, but whoever loses his life for my sake will find it" (v. 25). Jesus has come to save us, to be sure, and part of that work is saving us from ourselves.

C. S. Lewis famously wrote, "I didn't go to religion to make me happy. I always knew a bottle of Port would do that. If you want a religion to make you feel really comfortable, I certainly don't recommend Christianity."[5] That's one reason we end up with the devil as our professor. To make us uncomfortable. Not to learn evil but to learn how much evil is in us already. To realize how mightily we strive to save our lives, our selfish loves, from the grave in which they belong.

Our enemy below teaches us as only enemies can. The psalmist knew this well: "Before I was afflicted I went astray, but now I keep your word" (Ps. 119:67). And again, "It is good for me that I was afflicted, that I might learn your statutes" (v. 71). Until we feel those flaming arrows of the tempter, despair of saving ourselves, and stare in shock at the horror of what we are capable of, we still have much to learn.

More importantly, we discover in this classroom that the devil is teaching us against his will. He must do the Lord's bidding, not his own. What we learn, ultimately, is to mock the professor. When he throws our sins in our face, to say, "Yes, thank you for reminding me of that. Now I'll remind you that my Lord bled and died for that sin. It is no more. It was buried with Jesus but—unlike him—never saw the light of day again."

A strange thing transpires in this lecture hall: the weaker we become in ourselves, the stronger we become in Christ. The less we think of ourselves, the more love we have for others. The greater an awareness we have of our proclivity to immorality, the greater compassion we show to those who have been caught in adultery, stealing, lying, and murdering. Because we see in them but a reflection of ourselves. And because we see them through the eyes of Jesus, as those for whom he died.

Christ did not come to make us comfortable, happy, successful people. He came to conform us to himself by conforming us to his cross. To rip away the lies to which we cling and show us that true comfort, true joy, true love, are found only in the One who made us for himself. He's in no hurry to do this. He's with us for the long haul. And part of that time will be spent in the devil's classroom, enduring various losses and battles that we'd just as soon avoid. But

> We do not lose heart. Though our outer self is wasting away, our inner self is being renewed day by day. For this light momentary affliction is preparing for us an eternal weight of glory beyond all comparison, as we look not to the things that are seen but to the things that are unseen. For the things that are seen are transient, but the things that are unseen are eternal. (2 Cor. 4:16–18)

Discussion Questions

1. What is meant by a "professional religionist"? How and why does this sometimes happen to people? Do you agree or disagree with this statement: God is not a subject to be studied but the Lord to be worshiped. Why or why not?

_____

_____

_____

2. Review the life, sufferings, and eventual rise of Joseph, as recounted in Genesis 37-50. How does Psalm 105:16-22 interpret these events? What are some truths that we can learn from Joseph's experiences and apply to our own regarding suffering, God's absence/presence, and the (un)trustworthiness of our emotions?

_____

_____

_____

3.   In the quote from Martin Luther, he says that the devil is "the best teacher of theology." What does he mean? As you read through the summary of Chad's downfall, what were your thoughts about the devil's classroom? How does Luke 18:9-14 shed light on that statement, "You have to be dead to yourself to be resurrected in Jesus"?

_____

_____

_____

4.   What are some of the greatest blessings in your life? Did anything negative or painful make that list? Why are the Lord's blessings not so easy to spot? See Genesis 50:15-21 and Acts 2:22-24 for guidance.

_____

_____

_____

5.   In what way was Samson simultaneously the strongest and weakest of men? Read Judges 16:21-31 and Hebrews 11:32-34. What did Samson do at the end of his life and how was he a man of faith? Do you see any of yourself in Samson? Why are self-help spirituality and pep talks never enough to truly help us?

_____

_____

_____

6.   Read Matthew 16:24-25. Reflect on each of these three phrases: deny himself, take up his cross, follow me. What do they mean? How do you lose your life in Jesus and therefore find it?

_____

_____

_____

7.   Read Psalm 119:67 and 71. What do we learn from affliction about ourselves and about God? What do we learn about human evil and divine grace? If Jesus did not come to make us comfortable, when did he come to make us into? How does 2 Corinthians 4:16-18 give us hope as we are enrolled in the "devil's classroom"?

_____

_____

_____

Nine

Life in the Blood

With the patience and skill of a surgeon, he held the sharp penknife between his thumb and forefinger and began to cut a small square out of the printed page. He couldn't be rushed. This would take time. But he was a careful man, methodical in his plans as well as their execution. One cut down, one across, then down, then across. He leaned close to inspect the edges. Yes, nicely done. Neat, clean lines. Very carefully he lifted the two-inch square piece of paper, inked with words, and set it over to one side, where it joined scores of others. Some were larger, some smaller, but all were extracted from the same book. In time he would arrange and glue these pieces in sequence to form another, much shorter book. But for now that could wait. The dissection of this volume had just begun. When his task was complete, the pages of the original would be chock-full of gaps, like square and rectangular windows on an inked wall of paper.

All this happened about two hundred years ago. The book's surgeon was the principal author of the Declaration of Independence and the third president of the United States, Thomas Jefferson. And the volume he was dissecting was the Bible.

The shorter book Jefferson eventually created was titled *The Life and Morals of Jesus of Nazareth*, popularly known as the *Jefferson Bible*. It was a cut-and-paste Scripture. He arranged and glued the verses he'd extracted from the original into an abbreviated New Testament. Most noticeably missing are the miracles, including the resurrection. The Gospels end with Jesus still dead in the tomb. Jefferson, true to his deistic faith, rejected miraculous events as contrary to reason. His new book, gutted of the supernatural, was made in the image and likeness of his own philosophical assumptions. The *Jefferson Bible* tells us more about Jefferson than it does about the Bible.

Beyond its interest as a historical artifact of one man, the *Jefferson Bible* is a parable of sorts for all of us. It tells a story with a lesson as old as it is new. The story of subtracting Scripture according to preconceived notions of acceptability and plausibility. The story of what happens to God's Word when, guided by the spirit of the times, we hold a penknife between our thumb and forefinger to extract only those beliefs and practices we deem useful in today's world.

You won't find copies of the *Jefferson Bible* in the chairs or pews of any congregation, of course. But—let's be honest—you will discover its virtual equivalent. Our Bibles have verses, chapters, and sometimes even whole books that would hardly be missed if they were scissored out. Few if any sermons are based on them.

Sunday school students never study them. Bible classes aren't usually concerned with them. They are the parts of Scripture we often deem too esoteric to understand or too outdated to be relevant today.

Chief among these ignored sections are large swaths of the Old Testament, especially books like Leviticus. Chapters about holy tents, ritual worship, and gallons upon gallons of blood are from such a different time and culture that it hardly seems worth the effort to study them.

After all, why bother? What could these books possibly teach us today?

As it turns out, much more than we might think. The body of modern Christianity is by and large anemic. We sing and speak of power and glory but not so much the blood of the Lamb. We have a marked tendency toward spiritualizing and emotionalizing everything, as if we've forgotten that the beating heart of our faith is an actual beating heart. As Eugene Peterson writes, "Matter is real. Flesh is good. Without a firm rooting in creation, religion is always drifting off into some kind of sentimentalism or sophisticated intellectualism. . . . The Word did not become a good idea, or a numinous feeling, or a moral aspiration; the Word became flesh."[1] Blood and bones and skin are the very stuff of our salvation.

I routinely encounter believers who are taken aback, if not offended, when I emphasize that God is a flesh-and-blood man. You can take his pulse, touch his scars. Jesus is not a spirit, a messianic ghost flittering about the cosmos. He is divine, to be sure, but he is also fully and everlastingly human. Jesus didn't slough off his humanity on the day of his ascension. He took it with him. And he's never letting it go. Christ has skin in the game of our salvation, now and always.

The anemic New Testament church could use a transfusion of Old Testament blood. The earthiness of heaven, the humanness of God, the way our Lord is rooted in the concrete matter of this world—all of this is accented most strongly in those parts of Scripture we tend to Jeffersonize. In Scriptures like Leviticus, Exodus, and Numbers we find higher things anchored below. Tangible. Accessible. A drop of blood away. He tethers his promises of healing and peace and holiness not to the extraordinary but to the ordinary. He meets his people where they are, camps out among them, and even opens the door of his inner sanctum once a year. Frederick Buechner writes, "One of the blunders religious people are particularly fond of making is the attempt to be more spiritual than God."[2] The Old Testament rescues us from this spiritualization by showing us that the Lord is no aloof power barricaded in the sky. He's not the "man upstairs" but the God downstairs: boots on the ground, firmly where his people are, ready to serve and sanctify them.

Violent, Bad, Guilty Blood

This grounded, tangible God with salvation in his veins is precisely the kind of Savior our world needs. Echoing about, on a daily basis, are rival stories in a world hemorrhaging with evil.

Street violence between gangs paints the city asphalt red. Innocent blood spills at night clubs, malls, schools, and churches where terrorists unleash hate. We can't open our phones or turn on the radio without hearing a story involving carnage. The earth, which first opened its mouth to receive a brother's blood, has never stopped drinking in the life of victims (Gen. 4:11).

But the blood of violence is not the only story. There are the narratives of bad blood too. Deep fractures between races, nations, and within our families. Sons who haven't spoken to their fathers for years. Mothers who have disavowed their daughters. There are rifts within congregations and denominations that go back for decades. Bad blood, splintered relationships.

And there's blood guilt too. Some of us, no matter how often we scrub our hands, never completely efface the crimson stain. It's visible to us alone. Like a botched tattoo, it's always there, reminding us in ugly ways of what we've done. We carry the weight of innocent blood. It might have been an accident. It might have been on purpose. Whatever the cause, the result is the same: shame and regret shadow us through life.

All this blood. All this hurt. The fruit of violence, broken relationships, and shattered lives suffuses our world. It's everywhere. A pain not only personal and familial but national and global.

Such a massive problem, we might suppose, requires a solution just as big. Sweeping legal changes to deal with gun violence and drug trafficking. Government programs to address deeply seated racial prejudices. New leaders with fresh visions of a more just and equitable world. If we could only enact enough laws, rehabilitate enough people, and get the right programs in places, then we'd be well on our way to overcoming these challenges.

We might be. Or we might not be. Remember, none of our contemporary problems are all that contemporary. No evil, no prejudice, no pain just stepped onto the stage. All of humanity's struggles and vices—every single one of them—are ancient wounds. They've never healed. And that's not likely to change. Indeed, the biblical vision is not of humanity in gradual evolution but a devolving, ever-weakening demise. Listen to Paul's unoptimistic prophecy of humanity's future:

> In the last days there will come times of difficulty. For people will be lovers of self, lovers of money, proud, arrogant, abusive, disobedient to their parents, ungrateful, unholy, heartless, unappeasable, slanderous, without self-control, brutal, not loving good, treacherous, reckless, swollen with conceit, lovers of pleasure rather than lovers of God, having the appearance of godliness, but denying its power (2 Tim. 3:1–5).

Paul certainly didn't see the last days as the dawn of a new and improved humanity but as men and women *incurvatus in se*, as Augustine put it—turned in upon themselves, devouring each other and even themselves.[3]

Since our disease is so extreme, we naturally assume that God had better work in some amazing, profound ways to turn the tide. But the expectation of amazing, profound work by the Lord is itself part of our problem. We want God to act in some grandiose way. Maybe a cultural movement, fanned by his Spirit, sparking the flame of hope in the hearts of millions. Or a political or educational phenomenon inspiring a whole generation of young people to make the world a better place.

But, as we have repeatedly seen, Jesus is not a fan of the big and awesome. He's the messiah of the lowly manger and scandalous cross. The more people we see gathered around a common cause, the more electric the atmosphere, the more excitement is brewing in the hearts of people, the more we expect the Spirit to be present, effecting miraculous change. But that's not the divine way. Christ will be where he has promised to be. And he has promised to be where we, mesmerized by power and size, will never think to look for him. He's ensconced within the humble, the simple, the overlooked. And the gifts he offers will not be political, cultural, moral, or emotional in nature. They will be life itself. Life wet with blood. The kind of life that transforms our individual lives so that we become bearers of his life to the world.

Cowboys and Cancer

Jesus works slowly, individually, and tangibly when he interacts with people. And most of the time it goes completely unnoticed, except by those into whose death Christ pours forth life. People like Harvey.

Harvey and his sons, Randy and Rex, were farriers by trade. You might think of them as cowboy podiatrists of the equestrian world. They cared for the feet of horses. They drove their pickups all over Oklahoma, trimming hooves, pulling off old horseshoes and nailing on new ones. It's hard, dirty, sweaty, backbreaking labor, made even worse if the horse has a rebellious streak. When I was a teenager, I trimmed my own horse's hooves. I can't imagine doing it full-time. But Harvey and his sons did it, day in and day out.

That is, until the cancer came.

The kind of cancer you can attack with radiation or chemo, orthodox or unorthodox treatments, and it goes nowhere but forward. Advances with a relentless violence irrespective of the suffering of the patient. A kind of guerilla warfare that ambushes the body here and there until, finally, there's nothing left to do but stare at the clock and the calendar and await the inevitable end.

When I entered, the thick shades in the family room were pulled tight. Harvey was propped up on a makeshift bed. Ever the cowboy, he was wearing a faded pair of Wranglers.

"Thanks for coming," Harvey said.

"Glad to do it," I said.

"You got everything you need?"

"I do."

"Alright, then."

"Give me a second and we'll get started."

On the coffee table beside Harvey's bed I laid a piece of cloth, on top of which I placed a Bible, a small glass of wine, and a tiny silver dish with a wafer of bread on it.

I remember a few of the things I said to Harvey that day. I remember reading a psalm and a passage from the Gospels. We confessed our sins together, and I put my hand on his forehead and pronounced the Lord's forgiveness upon him. I spoke a few words to try and encourage him, assure him of God's mercy. And, having repeated what Jesus said in the upper room to his disciples, I took that piece of bread, held it to Harvey's mouth, and placed it inside, saying, "The body of Christ for you." And I took the glass of wine, held it to his lips, and let him drink it, saying, "The blood of Christ for you."

Yes, I remember a few of the things I said to Harvey that day. But I'll never forget what he said to me. As I prayed a final petition and prepared to leave, Harvey grabbed my hand, held it tight, and said, "Thank you, Lord, for coming to see me."

Out of the mouths of babes. And dying men. I don't know if I've ever had a moment of greater clarity in my life.

This is the way things are in the kingdom of God. Inside an Oklahoma farm-house, with a man days from death, the Lord was present not only to talk to him but to touch him, feed him, pour into his mouth the wine of new creation. It was like I wasn't even there. Only Jesus and Harvey. Only our Father and his child. One last time here on earth before that old cowboy rode away into a paradise awaiting him.

"Thank you, Lord, for coming to see me." Yes, Harvey, for so he comes. In shadowed rooms where cancer lurks. In lives on a collision course with the grave. He comes bearing gifts pregnant with life. Gifts we can feel and taste and smell. Tangible treasures. Little gifts full of big life—Christ's life. A life inextricably linked to the blood of death, the body of crucifixion, the very flesh of God.

The Lord came to see Harvey as he comes to see all of us, disguised as a beggar whose pockets bulge with gold.

Life in the Blood

It's a long trek from Harvey's country home to the foot of Mount Sinai, but that's really where that journey began. For it was there, during Israel's extended stay, that Yahweh gave us much of what is recorded in Exodus, Leviticus, and the beginning of Numbers. More specifically, it's there that God revealed why, when he comes to bless, heal, and vivify us, he always seems to have blood in tow.

In Leviticus 17:11, the Lord says, "For the life of the flesh is in the blood, and I have given it to you on the altar to make atonement for your souls; for it is the blood by reason of the life that makes atonement" (NASB). The context of this verse is vital for understanding what God is getting at. He is stating various prohibitions that relate to the proper and improper use of blood by Israel. Their pagan neighbors believed it was a life force they could manipulate. As OT scholar John Kleinig explains, "The blood of an animal was either drunk or, more commonly, eaten with its meat to gain its life-power, its vitality or health, its virility and fertility, its energy and strength."[4] To all that, God emphatically says *No*. No pouring out of blood in sacrifice to false gods (v. 7). No consumption of blood to harness some kind of spiritual power. Rather, blood was God's sole property to be used by his people only in ways he himself had ordained.

Notice four truths in verse 11: (1) Life was not some invisible force but a tangible element: "The life of the flesh is in the blood." (2) This liquid life was God's gift: "I have given it to you." (3) He located this life at a specific place: "on the altar." And (4) He gave it for a specific reason: "to make atonement for your souls." All of this is God's gift. He gives the life, he gives the altar, he gives the atonement. Sinners don't slice open their own veins to pay for their wrongdoing. Self-atonement is as impossible as self-birth or self-resurrection. A substitute must pay the price. The blood of another must be shed. And when it touches God's altar, the sacrificial blood covers God's people as a free gift to them.

The tabernacle of the Old Testament was not a slaughterhouse to satisfy the bloodthirst of an angry deity. It was the Father's house, where his children came to be redeemed by the death of a substitute. Here the Lord, via his priests, used blood as a sort of ritual detergent to cleanse them of every misdeed. Through daily and weekly sacrifices, as well as through offerings made on special days like Yom Kippur, the Lord forgave Israel, sanctified them, established peace with them, and kept them close to himself. And he did none of this without blood. As Hebrews would later say, "Indeed, under the law almost everything is purified with blood, and without the shedding of blood there is no forgiveness of sins" (9:22). We might be so bold as to add, "But *with* the shedding of blood, there is abundant forgiveness."

The more at home we become in books like Leviticus, the more we see how God comes to see us, as he came to see Harvey that day, not in intangibles but in solid, corporeal things. He is, after all, the Creator. He made lambs and oxen, men and women, bodies and blood. He doesn't blush over his creation, as if he's too good to get his hands dirty—or bloody. He doesn't stand in heaven and zap us with sanctity or telepathically communicate cleansing to us. Even life itself is not an abstract force for him but a bodily fluid. To see God's gifts, we don't stare up into the clouds; we turn our eyes down to the commonplaces of creation.

The longer we stay at Sinai, the more we are prepared for the Lord's ultimate stamp of approval on creation in his own corporality in Bethlehem. The Creator become creature. Is it such a great leap from God dwelling in the holy of holies to the God tabernacling in Mary's womb? From a tented Emmanuel to an bodied Emmanuel? The whole Old Testament prepares us for the Word becoming flesh.

Medicine of Immortality

Because the Son of God irrevocably united himself not just with this creation but with our very bodies, his acquaintance with our sufferings is not merely academic. He doesn't know our pains like one knows a chemistry formula. He knows what it's like to be one of us like Adam knew his wife. Intimately. Experientially. As one flesh. Knowing that encompasses the brain, the skin, the bowels, and the heart. God knows what it means to be loved and hated. Caressed and slapped. To fear for your life, be rejected by your family, mocked and laughed at. He is able to sympathize with our weaknesses because his muscles have been sore, his heart broken, his skin sweating blood (Heb. 4:15). He understands temptation because the devil's siren songs have reached his ears.

What's more, he also knows what it's like to feel shame and guilt and lust and revenge and disgust. Yes, even those. Because that's what he became when he sat down in the Roman electric chair as our substitute. The cross vacuumed every spot of wickedness off of us and sprayed it inside Jesus. No, he didn't sin. Something worse happened: he became sin. He became the rapist. He became the drug dealer. He became the child pornographer. He became the spiteful wife and the cheating husband. The unforgiving father and the hardened daughter. He became it all. He became us. He became The Sinner.

That's good news—but it's only half the gospel. You see, it does us no good to have a God who sympathizes with us, even a God who has taken away our sins, unless that same God comes to us with his gifts. Visits cowboys with cancer, teens with addictions, families with turmoil, and women riddled with guilt, to give us, one and all, what we need. And so he does. He walks the streets of violence, prisons, rehabilitation facilities, and bedrooms filled with the sobs of the forsaken. And he, the very embodiment of hope, pours that hope onto our parched lips. We taste and see that the Lord is good. He doesn't just remove the stained garments of our past; he clothes us with the white linen garments of a future with him. As the father did to his prodigal son, he brings out the best robe and puts a ring on our finger, sandals on our feet, and a fattened calf on the grill (Luke 15:22–23). Jesus didn't just become our sin; we became his righteousness. The full gospel is not just God taking away our evil; it's him giving us something better—healing grace—in its place.

This healing he does not through a wonder drug manufactured by a major pharmaceutical company. His elixir cannot be bought or sold, prescribed by doctors, or even purchased over the counter. It's free. Available to all. And distributed throughout the world every day without any fanfare. The blood of the Lamb, who takes away the sin of the world, takes this medicine of immortality to the sinners of the world. The life of God is in that blood, and he has given it to us on the altar of the cross to make atonement for our souls.

It doesn't seem like much. It's all wrapped up in outward simplicity. It flows through the veins of sermons and conversations between friends about Jesus and his love, and is mysteriously present in that sip of wine we drink from the Lord's table. But wherever it goes, the blood of Jesus leaves behind changed lives.

Such is its humble power that it was once able to take a pack of the most violent, bloodthirsty men in human history and transform them from wolves into lambs.

Wolves to Lambs

Henry Gerecke did what most ministers do when they arrive at a new congregation: he began introducing himself to the people he would be serving. He was as new to them as they were to him. So he made the rounds, shook hands, made sure to invite each of them to worship, and promised he'd be praying for them. There was nothing remarkable in all of this, of course. What was unusual, however, was that the people to whom he would be ministering were responsible for the worst genocide in human history.

Henry Gerecke was chaplain to the twenty-one Nazi prisoners who had formed the inner circle of Adolph Hitler.

At the close of World War II, Gerecke wanted nothing more than to go home. He had grown up with German-American parents on a farm in Missouri. After attending seminary, he did some work in St. Louis's jail system. When the war broke out and two of his sons went off to fight, Gerecke volunteered to be a chaplain, though he was almost fifty years old. His wife had been waiting two years for him back in the States. He had seen enough death and destruction to fill several lifetimes. But now, thank God, the carnage was over. The Allies were victorious. He could finally leave the blood-soaked soil of Europe behind.

But the military had other plans. They were in need of a bilingual Protestant chaplain, preferably one with experience in prison ministry, to serve the infamous German prisoners on trial at Nuremberg. So they approached Gerecke. Though he desperately wanted to return home, after praying over the decision, he walked back into his commander's office and spoke two words: "I'll go."[5]

Of course, the situation was hopeless. These men were the worst of the worst. Rudolf Hess, Hitler's deputy, who had helped him write *Mein Kampf*. Hermann Goering, Hitler's hand-picked successor. Joachim von Ribbentrop, the Führer's foreign minister. Wilhelm Keitel, his general field marshal and trusted military adviser. And many more. The innocent blood of millions was on their hands. Perhaps if they'd been reached earlier, there would be hope. But now they were well beyond the pale of salvation. Irredeemable. Unforgiveable. Even if, in our wildest imaginings, we could suppose there was some sliver of hope for any of these men, it would take a divine act of immense proportions to knock down the wall between God and them.

The wall between two prison cells had been knocked down. This small, Spartan space was the chapel. Inside were two candles, a makeshift altar, wooden benches, a small organ, and a crucifix on the wall. When Gerecke held his first service there, he had no idea what to expect. But it was packed. Thirteen prisoners squeezed inside the chapel. Thirteen of the most hated men in the world. Thirteen sinners whom many would have gladly thrown into hell with their own hands. Before them stood an ordinary chaplain. A short, middle-aged, bespectacled man of unimposing appearance. He had no grand vision of how to convert these men. He couldn't work miracles. All he had was a Bible, a sermon, some hymns, and a meal of bread and wine. It would take something infinitely more profound to transform the wolves of Hitler into the lambs of Christ.

So we would assume. But, as is most often the case when we are dealing with God's work, all our assumptions are dead wrong. As the months passed and the world watched as these criminals were put on trial, accused, convicted, and sentenced, something entirely different was happening behind the scenes.

Wilhelm Keitel, who had once written military reports and strategized attacks, now sat in his cell poring over his copy of the Scriptures every day. He and Gerecke spoke together a German prayer both their mothers had taught them as children. After several months of study, Keitel asked the chaplain if he could receive the Lord's Supper. And there, kneeling beside his cot, this former military commander, one of the most powerful leaders in the world, confessed his sins. Gerecke would later write, "On his knees and under deep emotional stress, [Keitel] received the Body and Blood of our Savior. . . . With tears in his voice he said, 'You have helped me more than you know. May Christ, my Savior, stand by me all the way. I shall need him so much.'"[6]

So it was with others. Three other prisoners, Albert Speer, Baldur von Schirach, and Hans Fritzsche, confessed the evils they had done, knelt before the crucifix in the chapel, and received from the chaplain's hand the tangible grace of Jesus.[7] So did Nazi labor chief Fritz Sauckel, who asked Gerecke how to prepare himself for the Lord's Supper, prayed with the chaplain, read the Bible, and even brought the catechism to court to read during the trial.[8] Not all of the men became believers, but little by little, through the steady, ordinary means of preaching, prayer, and the Supper of Jesus, the Spirit was doing the impossible. Saving the unsaveable. Redeeming the irredeemable. Forgiving the unforgivable. All through little things packed with immeasurable love.

In the middle of the night on October 16, 1946, Gerecke walked beside many of these same men to the gallows. One of them was Ribbentrop. Before they began that fateful walk, after they prayed in his cell, Ribbentrop told his pastor that "he put all his trust in the Blood of the Lamb that taketh away the sins of the world."[9] On top of the gallows, moments before he was hooded and the trapdoor would open to rope him into eternity, he turned to Gerecke and said, "I'll see you again."[10]

Sixteen years later, on another October day, far from Nuremberg, Germany, Henry Gerecke suffered a heart attack and died shortly afterward in the hospital. He was sixty-eight years old. I can't help but think that, when he was welcomed into paradise by the Lord whom he had served, he turned to see, all around him, the smiling faces of the men who had turned from the swastika to the cross. Whose sins the Lord remembered no more. Who washed their robes and made them white in the blood of the Lamb. I can almost hear them saying, "Welcome, home, Pastor Gerecke. We've been waiting for you."

An Ocean of Love

In a world full of increasing violence, rent asunder by racial ideologies and crippled by bloodguilt, it would seem we need huge solutions. No doubt, some small prog-ress is being made by individuals and groups laboring in governmental and social agencies to repair some aspects of broken humanity. But they can only do so much. Christ alone holds in his hands the medicine that works true and lasting peace in the hearts of the suffering, the depraved, the violent. Henry Gerecke knew that. We know that. We see the same story, over and over, from Genesis to Revelation.

Just as Jesus rode into Jerusalem on Palm Sunday, humbly, on the back of a donkey, so he comes riding into our lives, humbly, on the back of simple, unadorned gifts like words, water, bread, wine. He rode into Harvey's house that way to give him medicine that cured an ailment much worse than cancer. He rode into the prison cells of Keitel and Ribbentrop that way, bringing with him love that cured men the world deemed beyond help. And he rides to us, bearing the same gifts.

God, rooted and grounded in this creation, uses the elements of creation to fill us with joy and relief beyond description. Grapes grown from the soil, ripened, harvested, and fermented become the receptacle of the wine of heaven. We taste and see just how good the Lord is who comes to feed us, to quench our thirst, with himself.

His gifts may not look like much, but in one drop of Jesus's blood is an ocean of divine, healing love.

Discussion Questions

1. What was the Jefferson Bible and how does it function as a parable of sorts for us all? Which parts of the Bible do you rarely, if ever, hear preached about or taught in Bible class? Why do you think these are often ignored?

    _____

    _____

    _____

2. Eugene Peterson writes that "without a firm rooting in creation, religion is always drifting off into some kind of sentimentalism or sophisticated intellectualism." Elaborate on what that means. How can the earthiness of the Old Testament, especially with its focus on blood, free us from the danger of over-spiritualizing?

    _____

    _____

    _____

3. Read 2 Timothy 3:1-5. What is Paul's prognosis for human behavior as the world gets older and nearer to Christ's second coming? How does this match the common view that humanity—and worldly existence in general—is improving and evolving, that things are getting better? What is Christ's solution to our diseased and crumbling world?

    _____

    _____

    _____

4. The story about Harvey illustrates a vital truth. How does Christ visit us today? What does he bring with him? What does his blood give to us?

    _____

    _____

    _____

5.   Read Leviticus 17:11. Talk about the four (or more!) truths in this verse. What do the book of Leviticus and the worship at the tabernacle teach us about how the Lord comes to us? What are the solid, corporeal things in the church's worship today by which Christ blesses us with forgiveness, life, salvation?

   _____

   _____

   _____

6.   Read Hebrews 4:15, 2 Corinthians 5:21, and Galatians 3:10-14. What do these verses tell us about Christ's full participation in our humanity, and his full embrace of our sin? How does Jesus, having accomplished salvation for us, bring us that salvation in the here and now? What is the medicine of immortality?

   _____

   _____

   _____

7.   Discuss the story of Henry Gerecke and his ministry to Hitler's men. How did this chaplain minister to these men? How did they respond? What profound and comforting truths can we learn from how our Lord used the ministry of Gerecke? What hope does this give to those who say they are "too far gone" or "have done too much evil to be forgiven"?

   _____

   _____

   _____

Ten

Doing Nothing to the Glory of God

On that Christmas Day he had no idea how many "lasts" there would be. It was the last sermon he would preach in that congregation. The last day he would walk out of the warm sanctuary into the chilly Midwest air and drive away. The last time he would step inside his home, pack a suitcase, and leave on vacation with his family. So many unknown lasts on this first day of a life profoundly changed.

Dan Chambers had been one of my students at the seminary. A big, jovial guy with a comic streak and a knack for smoking sinfully delicious BBQ. After graduation, he relocated with his wife, son, and daughter to Manito, Illinois, where he took on the duties of the ministry. Late in 2011, after several weeks crammed with holiday services, children's programs, and parties, he was running on fumes. The nagging stomach issues he'd been suffering for some time exacerbated his exhaustion. But a vacation would rejuvenate him. All he needed was a little time away. After some R&R, he'd be back on his feet.

After fifteen hours on the road, they passed a sign that read, "Welcome to San Antonio, Texas." Instead of driving on to see family, however, they exited the freeway and pulled into the nearest hospital parking lot. Something was happening. The pain in Dan's abdomen was becoming unbearable. They parked the car and rushed inside the emergency room for help.

For one year, seven months, and four days, that hospital would be Dan's home.

Surgeon after surgeon would open him up to treat the gastronomical infection that had slowly been poisoning him. His prognosis would become so dire that, more than once, the doctors would tell his wife and children to prepare for the worst. Dan would be bedbound so long that hardened crystals would form around the joints in his hips and knees, restricting him to a wheelchair. His job at the church would end, along with the salary he needed to support his family. His wife, Karen, would scramble to find a new place to live, new schools for their children. For 580 days, my friend's world would shrink to a medical bed inside four antiseptic walls.

I stood within those four walls, beside that bed, many times over the course of his hospitalization. Dan and I would pray and read Scripture, but most of the time we'd simply talk. We'd talk about his family, how difficult it was to see Karen juggling so many challenges without him there beside her. How disheartening it was to miss his daughter's play, not to be there when his son took his driving test. We'd talk about his hobby, how he missed his BBQ Brethren, the group of men against whom he'd competed on so many Saturdays. And we'd talk about his ministry, how his inability to preach and teach was such a bitter pill to swallow. Though Dan did keep a remarkably upbeat view of life despite his sufferings, there was still that undercurrent of frustration at not being able to work, to do the labor for which the Lord had equipped him. He'd wanted a week-long vacation, not a nineteen-month sabbatical from all the duties and responsibilities that had defined his life as a husband, father, and pastor.

Let's return to Dan's story in a minute. But first, let's talk about work, rest, and the occupational hazard that follows us into every job.

What Do You Do for a Living?

When we're becoming acquainted with people, one of the stock questions we usually ask them is "What do you do for a living?" But it's more than a polite, innocent query. There are a hundred unspoken little interrogatives creeping inside that single question: Where do you work? What specifically is your job there? What are you tasked with accomplishing on a daily basis? What kind of training and degrees were necessary to land that position? Where does it locate you on the implicit social scale operative in American society? Is it blue collar or white collar? How does it compare to our job, our salary, our upward mobility? And so on. If Gerald says, "I'm a senior project manager for an investment banking firm," and Tom says, "I work part-time at Burger King," in a split second do we not adopt, almost unconsciously, countless assumptions about the relative importance Gerald and Tom have in life?

When we ask, "What do you do for a living?" what we're really asking is, "Is there anything extraordinary about you that we need to know?"

This is an embarrassing truth to admit, but one that reveals something about how we judge people. We tend to pigeonhole others based upon what they do. How much they contribute to society. How much money they make. We have a sophisticated algorithm in our minds that calculates, within a millisecond of a person's revelation of their occupation, how significant a human being they are. And it's all based upon the shallowest of criteria: what they do from nine to five.

Our jobs, our labor, are indeed a gift of God. Even before the advent of evil in the world, Adam was a gardener, placed in Eden to "work it and keep it" (Gen. 2:15). "There is nothing better than that a man should rejoice in his work," Ecclesiastes says (3:22). Paul tells the believers in Thessalonica, "Work with your hands . . . so that you may walk properly before outsiders and be dependent on no one" (1 Thess. 4:11–12). In a later letter to this same congregation, he criticized those who were idle, "not busy at work, but busybodies" (2 Thess. 3:11). He reminded them of what he'd said while he was there, "If anyone is not willing to

DOING NOTHING TO THE GLORY OF GOD

work, let him not eat" (v. 10). Shunning laziness, they are "to do their work quietly and to earn their own living," and never "grow weary in doing good" (v. 13). Just as God labored six days in his job of creation, so men and women, formed in his image and likeness, faithfully do their labor. Make their living. Bring home the bacon. Pay the bills. And help others in need.

But with our jobs, as with all the gifts of God, we tend to twist things around. We unwrap these gifts, disassemble them, and reassemble the parts into something like an ego-expanding machine. We turn labor into an ugly tool for accomplishing the very opposite of what God intended. Instead of our jobs serving our neighbors in love, we use them to keep up with the Joneses—or, if we have our way, to pass up the Joneses. Work morphs into one of the gods in our personal pantheon that we can manipulate in our ambitious quest to rise to the top, look down our noses at those less fortunate, and collect all the toys that invest our lives with meaning. Instead of thinking of our jobs as a table where we can feed others, they become barns in which we horde our treasures.

But what happens when, like my friend, Dan, we can't work? We're injured and forced into a period of convalescence? We get laid off or fired and no one will hire us? It eats away at our sense of self-worth. We must be achieving something to matter, preferably something above average. I realize there is a deep psychological need here, but there's also a theological reality at play. We begin to think God is like us; that he, too, determines the significance of a human being based upon how much they produce.

So our Father does what he always does: he intervenes to save us from ourselves. He steps in front of us while we're on the way up to build bigger barns or on the way down the hillside of despondency. He picks us up and places us in the nearest chair.

Sit, he says.

But I've got things to do.

Stop.

But I feel worthless when I don't accomplish anything.

Silence.

But I have deadlines, commitments, quotas, dreams, aspirations, ambitions.

Rest.

But I'll fall behind my competitors.

Sit. Hush. Rest.

If any of the Spirit's jobs really makes him work up a sweat, it must be the arduous task of getting us to do nothing. To stop worrying about making more money. To stop making plans for the next accomplishment. To stop fretting about all the things we must do in our ongoing crusade to justify ourselves before God and others. The Spirit works hard simply to get us to sit at the feet of Jesus, take a deep breath, and not do anything but rejoice in the Sabbath rest of Christ's accomplished work.

The Forgotten Day of Creation

When I was a boy, my grandfather and I would wait for the sun to sink below the western horizon, wait a little longer for the woods near my home to be cloaked in darkness, then strike out. With a lantern, a .22 rifle, and three dogs, we'd head for the trees. The hounds had one thing on their minds: raccoons. They'd go hog wild. They'd zigzag through the trees, noses glued to the ground, scanning for the scent that would eventually have them—if we were lucky—baying triumphantly at the foot of an oak. Two yellow eyes on a bandit face would gleam angrily down from one of the branches.

But that might take hours. In the meantime, he and I walked. And we walked. Up and down hills, over muddy creeks, pushing our way through thick brush. My grandfather was a spry man who never seemed to get winded. I, on the other hand, scampered along on short legs, huffing and puffing, trying my best to keep up. About every hour or so, he would stop, set the lantern down near a fallen log, and say, "You know, I think I need a break. These dogs are wearing me out."

He wasn't quite telling the truth. I was the one breathing hard, not him. But I was too proud to complain about my exhaustion. So my grandfather, seeing what I needed, took the initiative. He sat on the log so I could sit beside him. He, who needed no rest, took a rest so that I, who needed rest, could catch my breath before we moved on.

There are lessons about God to be learned in all sorts of places, even deep in the woods, on summer nights, when a little boy and his grandfather sit side by side, listening to hounds baying in the distance. Here was a Sabbath lesson.

On the seventh day of creation, the Lord finally punched the time clock. All his work was done. And it was good, very good. He blessed that final day. Made it holy. And on that seventh day he "rested from all his work that he had done in creation" (Gen. 2:3). He wasn't breathing hard. He wasn't worn out from laying the foundations of the earth, shutting the doors of the seas, and filling the storehouses with snow. He was just finished. But he still stopped, took a seat, and rested for a whole day.

He rested so that Adam and Eve, his son and daughter, could sit beside him, as I had beside my grandfather. They rested with him. Because he knew, as only a father can, that his children would need their rest. They couldn't labor nonstop, seven days a week. And if they tried, they would easily forget one of the fundamental truths about being human: that we have limitations. As the Jewish scholar Nahum Sarna writes, "[Man] rediscovers his own very human dimension, his earthliness, for the Sabbath delimits human autonomy."[1] We rediscover our human dimension as we rest. We are not God. Our short legs and mortal hearts can only take us so far. And if we try to push past that boundary, we don't become more human—we become less.

One of the lessons we've seen repeatedly is that God works in our lives by working undercover. By concealing himself underneath the simple. And in so doing undermining our presuppositions about where he is found. We find him with friends in low places, in godforsaken deserts, in anonymous saints, and in the blood of the Lamb that takes away the sin of the world. We also find him resting.

And he commands us to be copycats. "Remember the Sabbath day, to keep it holy," he says (Exod. 20:8). The only day in creation God called holy is the one on which he commanded us to do nothing. Implicit in that command is that holiness is a gift, not an achievement. On that day we remember that being human does not mean doing great things for God and thereby becoming holy. It means resting in the great work of Christ, who makes us holy, who is our sanctification (1 Cor. 1:30). He has done all the labor for our salvation, has waged and won our battles for us. In him we who haven't conquered anything on our own become more than conquerors (Rom. 8:37).

When Every Earthly Prop Gives Way

We need to learn this lesson over and over, as did our Israelite brothers and sisters. And never did God give them—and us—a more memorable object lesson about resting and letting him fight our battles than on the shore of the Red Sea.

In one stanza of the old hymn, "My Hope Is Built on Nothing Less," we sing of those times "when every earthly prop gives way."[2] Those six words would be the perfect caption for the snapshot of Israel in Exodus 14. At their backs was the Blitzkrieg of Egypt, led by its iron-hearted monarch, thirsty for blood to avenge the death of their firstborn sons. In front of them the waters of the sea lapped the shore. Either way, they were dead men walking. Every earthly prop gave way for Israel that day.

They didn't realize it, but God had led them right where he wanted them. Out of options—save him alone. Out of avenues of escape—save him alone. When we stand surrounded by forces outside our control, when no amount of sweat or street smarts can rescue us, then Christ has room to act. This is the Sabbath of faith, where we trust that Christ will fight while we're fatigued, save while we snore, do everything while we do nothing but kick back and watch.

"Fear not," Moses told the weak-kneed Israelites. "Stand firm, and see the salvation of the LORD, which he will work for you today" (Exod. 14:13).

Eugene Peterson captures the thrust of the words that follow: "God will fight the battle for you. And you? You keep your mouths shut!" (v. 14 Message).

Don't work yourselves into a frenzy. Don't jack your jaws about what a stupid idea it was to leave Egypt. Don't do anything. Just sit on that sandy beach for a minute. God's got this saving thing down pat. He doesn't need your help. Take a deep breath. Keep your mouths shut. Rest.

Is there any harder position for us to be in than this? Nothing scares us more than losing control. Turning things completely over to someone else, even if that someone else is God—*especially* if that someone else is God. For there's no telling what he might do. He is the God whose actions unnerve us because they're so wrongheaded. He is, after all, the God who sent Gideon into battle with trumpets and torches, who armed Moses with only a stick—who, when he calls a person to follow him, "bids him come and die," in Dietrich Bonhoeffer's memorable words.[3] As odd as it sounds, the hardest day of creation for us to accept is the Sabbath, for that day drives home the point that we are not in control. It's all up to God, the God who creates everything—including our rescue—out of nothing.

There's an old Jewish legend that says the Red Sea did not split open until the Israelites stepped into the waters and waded out to where "the waters reached up to their very noses." Then and only then did the waters part and dry land appear.[4] But this legend gives way too much credit to the Israelites. They didn't courageously step out in faith; they stood there in silence, waiting and watching, until God "drove the sea back by a strong east wind all night and made the sea dry land, and the waters were divided" (v. 21). Israel did nothing. And God, from nothing, did everything for them.

But, to use Bonhoeffer's phrase, he did bid them "come and die." He does so with us on our own Red Sea shores, when we feel trapped by uncontrollable forces that threaten to undo us. Come, die to doubt and unbelief. Die to always being in control. Take up the cross of faith and find therein life. A life full of joyous surprises from the God who shows up when every earthly prop gives way and leads us through a way in the sea, a path in the great waters, though his footprints are unseen (Ps. 77:19).

Sit on Your Hands and Know That I Am God

The deliverance at the Red Sea is a sort of narrative commentary on one of the most subversive verses in the Bible: "Be still, and know that I am God" (46:10). The Hebrew verb variously translated as "be still" (ESV), "cease striving" (NASB), or "let be" (JPS Tanakh) is *raphah*. It means to sink down or let something drop, commonly the hands (e.g., Neh. 6:9). And, as we have seen before, "know" (*yada*) is not merely a mental grasp of a subject but an experiential participation in something. With that in mind, we might summarize the psalm verse this way: "I don't want you to lend me a hand or take matters into your own hands. Rather, sit on your hands and experience the reality of what it means for me to be your God."

This is all the more significant when we consider the rest of Psalm 46. Far from being a time of relative calm, the earth is giving way and the mountains are slipping into the heart of the sea. Nations are raging and kingdoms tottering. All hell is breaking loose. If there were ever a time to sit on our hands, this is certainly not it. We need to act. Form a committee. Implement a plan to stem the tide of disaster. Keep our hands busy 24/7 until we figure out a way to achieve whatever needs to be done. But the Lord subverts our schemes, overthrows them with this verse: "Be still, and know that I am God."

Yes, of course, there are times when God calls us to act. The Scriptures are full of admonitions to defend the widow and the orphan, to feed the hungry, to speak out for those who have no voice. Christianity is not a faith of do-nothing passivism that shrugs at the sufferings of the needy. But neither is it a faith that believes activism is the key to the world's problems—or our personal and family problems, for that matter. There is a time to work and a time to rest. A time to use our hands for good and a time to sit on them. But if modern Christianity gravitates too far in either direction, it's the way of doing. We live by the unbiblical creed "Be busy, and know that God is impressed."

The patron saints of modern Christianity are those who have achieved fame by accomplishing great things, by not sitting on their hands. Leaders who advocate "vision casting," who dream big, plan big, and go on to achieve big success in various ministries. The founders of megachurches with attendees so numerous only a converted sports stadium can seat them all. They are also NFL players and musical stars who, being famous Christians, are held up as role models for young people. The common bond among these iconic elites is that they have achieved the spiritual equivalent of the American dream. Thus, to the modern mind, this alone invests them with sacred authority, invites emulation, and says, "Now there's someone who's done great things for the glory of God. Go and do likewise."

Instead of looking up to famous, successful saints such as these, it would be better to turn our eyes downward, to consider how God is at work in the lives of believers who have learned, on the shores of their own Red Sea, during times of Sabbath rest, to sit on their hands and experience the reality of what it means for God to be their God—people like my friend Dan Chambers.

The Gospel Is Not Disabled

On a corner lot on the west side of San Antonio sits a modest home with a smoker and grill in the backyard, a special-equipped van parked out front, and a ramp leading up to the front door. When you walk inside and pass through the family room, you step into the kitchen with a seating area off to one side. There you will find a man in a wheelchair, smiling at you. How does he smile, you might wonder, after all he's been through? Perhaps you'll have some inkling when you hear the rest of his story.

In August 2013, after 580 days in the hospital, the time had finally arrived. Dan was going home—though he'd be going to a home he hadn't seen until that day. He could no longer walk. There was a wound in his abdomen that still had not fully healed. His hair had thinned. But he was still alive. And he was leaving the hospital with his wife, son, and daughter by his side.

For the two years following, Dan would be in and out of rehabilitation facilities, where physical therapists would work to restore strength and movement to his legs. Some modest progress would be made, but it largely seemed a one-step-forward-two-steps-back kind of progress. He also returned to the hospital for several follow-up surgeries.

During those two years, whenever I drove away from one of our visits at his home or in a medical facility, the single consistent impression I had was not one of pity, or even of sympathy. It was admiration. I don't mean admiration for how tough and courageous Dan was—though he has those qualities in spades—nor even for how optimistic he was in the face of such daily, daunting challenges. I mean a kind of profound, almost shocked admiration for the fact that he was more concerned about others than he was about himself. He was concerned about his family. He sent encouraging emails to his fellow believers. He prayed for every friend he knew was in need. Here was a man who had suffered, in a few short years, more than most of us will suffer in a lifetime. Yet the first words out of his mouth were always "How are you doing?" instead of "Woe is me."

The fact that you are holding this book in your hands is largely because of him. For several years, I had given up on writing. When Dan and I first met, I was a professor who contributed regularly to magazines and journals and was busily writing an academic book. During the intervening years, after my career and marriage imploded, I locked my pen inside a box of fear. No more writing for me. I was damaged goods anyway. A washed-up failure with no words to contribute anymore. Dan saw me differently than I saw myself. He looked at me through eyes of grace. Not once, in our many conversations, did he pry into or dig up my past sins. Not once did he treat me as anything but a forgiven, beloved brother. And one Saturday afternoon, as we talked together in his hospital room, he told me, with the authority of a man who cannot be ignored, that it was high time for me to unlock that box of fear, take out my pen, and get back to work.

As you can see, I did.

On November 29, 2015, almost four years after Dan preached his last sermon in Illinois, my family and I drove east out of San Antonio. We passed by the town of Seguin and used back roads to get to a rural community named Kingsbury. On the edge of town we pulled into the gravel parking lot of a small church. A man in a cowboy hat was standing outside, shaking hands and extending that famous southern hospitality to one and all. One of the elders greeted us warmly as we walked in and ushered us to a pew. The organ finished its prelude. It was time for the service to begin.

But this was no ordinary service. A door opened and rolling into view was a man in a wheelchair. He was wearing a white robe. He was smiling. His voice was full and strong. Here was the new under-shepherd of this small, faithful flock of the Good Shepherd. Here was a man fully schooled in the theology of the cross, who had learned to be still and know that God is God, and who realized the limitations of his humanity. Here was Dan Chambers, ready to be officially welcomed and installed as pastor of Evangelists Lutheran Church.

I don't know about you, but when I want to look up to someone who's learned what it means to sit at the feet of Jesus, I don't look up to the famous, the iconic, the hyper-achievers. I look down upon humble, broken believers like my friend Dan, who have discovered, in their deficiencies and limitations, the Spirit of the God who fills them with the fullness of grace in the One who embodies Sabbath rest.

Come unto Me

"Come unto me," Jesus says, "all ye that labour and are heavy laden, and I will give you rest. Take my yoke upon you, and learn of me; for I am meek and lowly in heart: and ye shall find rest unto your souls. For my yoke is easy, and my burden is light" (Matt. 11:28–30 KJV).

Come unto me, all who labor under the heavy burden of trying to justify your existence by outperforming everyone else, and I will be your Sabbath rest. I will give you the peace that passes understanding, the peace of knowing that, in me, your warfare is ended, your iniquity is pardoned, and you have received from the Lord's hand a doubling of grace for all your sins (Isa. 40:2).

Come unto me, all who bear the heavy load of trying to live up to the bigger, better, bolder demands of a society that defines self-worth by accomplishments, and I will be your Sabbath rest. I will show you that the meek shall inherit the earth, the last shall be first, and the humble shall be exalted.

Come unto me, all who feel trapped on the shores of the Red Sea, who think their lives are at an end, who see no way out, and I will be your Sabbath rest. I will open a way through the sea, I will love you back into hope again, and I will show you that no one is more precious and important to me than you.

Come unto me, all you anonymous saints, the forgotten ones who've slipped through the cracks in the world, who feel invisible, and I will be your Sabbath rest. For I know you by name, have placed my name upon you, and pray for you by name at the throne of my Father.

Come unto me, high and low, popular and unpopular, educated and uneducated, one and all, and I will be your Sabbath rest. I am hidden yet fully present in the world. I am glorious yet lowly in heart. And in my heart there is more than enough room for the world.

Discussion Questions

1. Read Genesis 2:15, Ecclesiastes 3:22, 1 Thessalonians 4:9-12, and 2 Thessalonians 3:11-12. Taken together, what do these verses tell us about work? Is labor a gift of God or a result of the fall into sin?

2. Think about conversations you have had with someone about what they and you do for a living. What kind of assumptions and prejudices often arise during those conversations? What does this tell us about ourselves? Why do we put so much emphasis on a person's job, as if that fact defines them as a person?

3. Discuss this quote: "If any of the Spirit's jobs really makes him work up a sweat, it must be the arduous task of getting us to do nothing." What is meant by this? Why do we find it so difficult to stop making money, making plans, doing things?

4. Read Genesis 2:1-3 and Exodus 20:8-11. What set apart the seventh day as special? How did the Old Testament Sabbath day help people to rediscover their human dimension and limit their autonomy? How does rest do that same for us today?

5.   Read Exodus 14:1-14. Why did the Lord lead the Israelites into a location where they were out of options? Why do we rebel against losing control of situations in which we find ourselves? How is Christ at work in those situations when every earthly prop gives way?

_____

_____

_____

6.   Read Psalm 46. What is happening in this psalm? What kind of language is used to describe the undoing of creation? Given this context, why is verse 10 all the more remarkable? How do we, as Christians, achieve balance between active and being still?

_____

_____

_____

7.   Do you know someone like Dan Chambers, someone who has learned what it means to sit at the feet of Jesus? What can we learn from them and their example?

_____

_____

_____

8.   Read Matthew 11:28-30. Based on these words, describe what kind of Savior we have in Jesus. How is he our Sabbath rest?

_____

_____

_____

Notes

Chapter 1 God Hiding in Plain Sight

1. In his excellent book *Ordinary: Sustainable Faith in a Radical, Restless World*, Michael Horton devotes chapter 5 to discussing how ambition went from being a vice to a virtue (Grand Rapids: Zondervan, 2014), 87–103.

2. Brennan Manning, *Abba's Child: The Cry of the Heart for Intimate Belonging* (Colorado Springs: NavPress, 2015), preface to the 2002 edition, xvii.

3. Thomas Hobbes, *Leviathan*, vol. 23 of *Great Books of the Western World*, ed. Robert M. Hutchins (Chicago: University of Chicago, 1952), 85.

4. Manning, *Abba's Child*, xvii.

Chapter 2 Friends in Low Places

1. For this insight I am indebted to A. J. Swoboda, who discusses Jesus's amazement in *A Glorious Dark: Finding God in the Tension between Belief and Experience* (Grand Rapids: Baker, 2015), 177.

Chapter 3 Godforsaken Hangouts

1. Robert Capon, *Kingdom, Grace, Judgment: Paradox, Outrage, and Vindication in the Parables of Jesus* (Grand Rapids: Eerdmans, 2002), 452.

2. Tikhon Shevkunov, *Everyday Saints and Other Stories*, trans. Julian H. Lowenfeld (Dallas: Pokrov Publications: 2012), chapter on "Father Gabriel."

3. Ibid.

Chapter 4 Unorthodox Headhunter

1. Nadia Bolz-Weber, *Accidental Saints: Finding God in All the Wrong People* (New York: Convergent Books: 2015), 39.

2. John Kleinig, *Grace Upon Grace: Spirituality for Today* (St. Louis: Concordia Publishing House, 2008), 63–64.

Chapter 5 Bringing a Knife to a Gunfight

1. As quoted by Jean Danielou, S. J., *The Bible and the Liturgy* (Notre Dame: University of Notre Dame Press, 1956), 41.

2. There are, of course, a variety of teachings about baptism in the church. Some understand this verse to refer to spiritual baptism, others to water baptism. Rather than an either/or, a both/and fits well here. Water baptism is the baptism of the Spirit. He is active in the water with his Word to unite us to Christ and his saving work.

3. William H. C. Propp calls the staffs of Moses and Aaron the "projections onto the terrestrial plane of Yahweh's incorporeal arm" in his commentary, *Exodus 1–18: A New Translation with Introduction and Commentary*, vol. 2 of *The Anchor Bible* (New York: Doubleday, 1998), 229.

4. R. J. Grunewald, *Reading Romans with Luther* (St. Louis: Concordia Publishing House, 2016), 35.

5. Tish Harrison Warren, *Liturgy of the Ordinary: Sacred Practices in Everyday Life* (Downers Grove, IL: IVP Books, 2016), 19.

Chapter 6 Saints John and Jane Doe

1. Henri J. M. Nouwen, *Life of the Beloved: Spiritual Living in a Secular World* (New York: The Crossroad Publishing Company, 2002), 33.

Chapter 7 Unsexy Church

1. English translations render the phrase as "a man, the LORD," as "a man with the help of the LORD" (ESV), or as "with the help of the LORD I have brought forth a man" (NIV). The Hebrew particle *eth*, which is placed before "the LORD," can either mark the definite accusative or mean "with" or "together with." OT scholar Walter C. Kaiser Jr. writes, "Perhaps Eve thought Cain was [that male descendant promised in Gen 3:15]. She named her son Cain saying that she had 'gotten a man, even the Lord' (Gen. 4:1); at least, that is one way of rendering this enigmatic phrase." *Toward an Old Testament Theology* (Grand Rapids: Zondervan, 1978), 79.

2. C. S. Lewis, *The Screwtape Letters* (New York: Macmillan, 1961), 116.

3. Ibid., 119.

4. Jen Pollock Michel, *Teach Us to Want: Longing, Ambition and the Life of Faith* (Downers Grove, IL: IVP Books, 2014), 64.

5. James K. A. Smith, *You Are What You Love: The Spiritual Power of Habit* (Grand Rapids: Brazos Press, 2016), 67.

6. Ibid., 23.

7. Michael Horton, *Ordinary: Sustainable Faith in a Radical, Restless World* (Grand Rapids: Zondervan, 2014), 35.

8. Kate Hankey, William G. Fischer, "I Love to Tell the Story," 1866, 1869.

9. Martin Luther, *Lectures on Genesis: Chapters 6–14*, vol. 2 of *Luther's Works*, American edition (St. Louis: Concordia Publishing House, 1960), 334.

10. Ibid.

Chapter 8 Learning about God in the Devil's Classroom

1. "Love Comes from the Other Side of Town," *Does Fort Worth Ever Cross Your Mind*, MCA Records, 1984.

2. As quoted by John Kleinig in "Oratio, Meditatio, Tentatio: What Makes a Theologian?" *Concordia Theological Quarterly* 66/2 (2002), 255–67, emphasis mine.

3. Chad Bird, *Night Driving: Notes from a Prodigal Soul* (Grand Rapids: Eerdmans, 2017).

4. Johnson Oatman Jr., "Count Your Blessings," 1897.

5. C. S. Lewis, "Answers to Questions on Christianity," *God in the Dock* (New York: HarperOne, 2014), 58.

Chapter 9 Life in the Blood

1. Eugene H. Peterson, *The Contemplative Pastor: Returning to the Art of Spiritual Direction*, vol. 17 in *The Leadership Library* (Carol Stream, IL: Word Publishing, 1989), 77.
2. Frederick Buechner, *Wishful Thinking: A Theological ABC* (New York: Harper and Row, 1973), 43.
3. For an in-depth treatment of the meaning and origin of the phrase *incurvatus in se*, along with its popular manifestations in modern life, see Heather Choate Davis, *Man Turned In On Himself: Understanding Sin in 21st-Century America* (Icktank Press, 2014).
4. John Kleinig, *Leviticus*, vol. 2 in *Concordia Commentary* (St. Louis: Concordia Publishing House, 2003), 365.
5. For the quotes and background about Gerecke, I am indebted to Tim Townsend, who documents the story in *Mission at Nuremberg: An American Army Chaplain and the Trial of the Nazis* (New York: HarperCollins, 2014), 105. See also F. T. Grossmith, *The Cross and the Swastika* (Boise, ID: Pacific Press Publishing Association, 1984).
6. Townsend, *Mission at Nuremberg*, 11.
7. Ibid., 181.
8. Ibid., 174.
9. Ibid., 271.
10. Ibid., 272.

Chapter 10 Doing Nothing to the Glory of God

1. Nahum Sarna, *Genesis*, vol. 1 of *The JPS Torah Commentary* (Philadelphia: The Jewish Publication Society, 1989), 15.
2. Edward Mote, "My Hope Is Built on Nothing Less," 1834.
3. Dietrich Bonhoeffer, *The Cost of Discipleship* (New York: Collier Books, 1963), 99.
4. Hayim N. Bialik and Yehoshua H. Ravnitzky, eds., *The Book of Legends*, trans. William G. Braude (New York: Schocken Books, 1992), 73.

Subject Index

Jeremiah, on stubbornness of Israel, 15

Jericho, theologian in Jericho brothel, 14–15

Jerusalem, 75; Jesus Christ entrance into, 106; pilgrimages to, 32–33

Jesus Christ: as among the common, 21; armor of, 58–59, 60; baptism and identity in, 60; baptism of, 55; becoming strong in, 93–94; calling the laborers to himself, 117; centurion's belief in, 18–19, 24; the church and, 82, 84; crucifixion of, 36; dependence on, 44–45; as embodiment of hope, 103; entrance into Jerusalem, 106; family tree of, 15, 20, 77–78, 85; forty days in the wilderness, 36; as hidden God, 64; Isaiah's prophecies about, 8; mind of, 80; pace of work in our lives, 78–79; parable of the rich man, xi; parable of the sheep and the goats, 26; as tabernacle-in-the-flesh, 75–76; tempted by Satan, 55; trust in, 41; unbelief of Jews of Nazareth in, 18–19, 24; who became sin, 103, 108; in the wilderness, 7. *See also* the Messiah

John the Baptist, 69

John the Evangelist, Saint, 82

Jonah, 48; mission of, 41–43

Joppa, 42

Joseph (son of Jacob): blessings of, 91; dreams of, 88; suffering of, 87–89, 94

Joshua, 14–15

Judah (son of Jacob), 77

Judean wilderness, as Godforsaken place, 10

Kaiser, Walter C., Jr., 122n1(ch7)

Keitel, Wilhelm, 104, 105, 106

king of the double-wide trailer, 16–18, 22, 24

kingdom of God, as hidden in simplicities, 8–9

Kleinig, John, 40, 48, 102

knife to a gunfight: discussion questions, 59–61; Gideon's brass band and pottery class, 52–53; liquid armor of God, 55–56; running as a weapon, 50–51; staff of God, 56–59; true enemies, 53–55

labor: as gift from God, 110; reason for, 118; salvation and, 113

lackluster people and places, God as active in, 6

language of heaven, 85

Lazarus, xi

learning about God in devil's classroom: count your blessings or count your crosses, 90–92; devil's classes on freedom, pleasure, independence, 89–90; discussion questions, 94–96; dreams becoming nightmares, 87–89; in Indiana, 86–87; Samson, 92–93; uncomfortable Christianity, 93–94

leprosy: healing of, 11; of Naaman, 6, 11, 66–68, 67, 72; unorthodox healing remedies for, 7

Lewis, C. S., 93

life in the Blood: cowboys and cancer, 100–101; discussion questions, 107–8; Jefferson, 97–98; life in the blood, 101–2; medicine of immortality, 103–4; ocean of love, 106; violent, bad, guilty blood, 98–100; wolves to lambs, 104–6

Life of the Beloved (Nouwen), 64

listening, to works of God, xi

Liturgy of the Ordinary (Warren), 59

loneliness, 71

longing, in the wilderness, 10

loss of identity, as spiritual malady, 7

Lot, 19

love, of God the Creator, 7

low place friends: dumpster sermon, 21; profound faith of, 21–22; Ruth and, 24

lowliness, God in, 7

Luther, Martin, 83, 89, 95

Scripture Index

SCRIPTURE INDEX

SCRIPTURE INDEX

SCRIPTURE INDEX

Chad Bird is a Scholar in Residence at 1517. He holds master's degrees from Concordia Theological Seminary and Hebrew Union College. He has served as a pastor, professor, and guest lecturer in Old Testament and Hebrew. Chad has authored several books, speaks regularly at conferences and congregations, and cohosts the popular podcast, "40 Minutes in the Old Testament." Chad and his wife Stacy make their home in Texas, where they have been blessed with four children and three grandchildren.